A Homemade World

Alfred A. Knopf   New York   1975

A Homemade World

The American Modernist

Writers ✒ by Hugh Kenner

Library of Congress Cataloging in Publication Data

Kenner, Hugh   A homemade world.
1. American literature—20th century—History
and criticism.   I.   Title.
PS221.K4   810'.9'005   74-7759
ISBN 0-394-49102-5

for Guy Davenport

Contents

Acknowledgments

An earlier version of the substance of Chapter IV has appeared in *The Southern Review* (Autumn 1965) under the title "The Experience of the Eye: Marianne Moore's Tradition." A few paragraphs in Chapter VI are adapted from part of my review of Louis Zukofsky's *"A"* in *Poetry* (November 1967). The book has benefited throughout from notes made on an earlier version by Maynard Mack and Arthur Mizener.

Introductory

"Old father, old artificer," Stephen Dedalus called into the winds of time and space, "stand me now and ever in good stead." Raised a Catholic, he is praying to his name-saint, but not a saint on the calendar of the Irish church: to the "hawklike man" of an older religion still: to Dedalus who made the labyrinth and made wings.

Dedalus had made wings because after he had made the labyrinth the Cretans were unwilling to let the deviser of its secret leave their island. As for the labyrinth, he had made it to contain the Minotaur. The Minotaur needed containing because it was the unnatural get of a Cretan bull on Queen Pasiphae, who had one night satisfied her sexual whim with the aid of an apparatus Dedalus constructed for her.

So that had been his seminal piece of devising, that wooden cow to contain Queen Pasiphae's yearning tissues: a technology which obligated further technologies, the labyrinth, the wings. (The wings were to cost him his son, which flawed the sequence of triumphs. Yet the classical deduction was not that technologies breed death, but that sons should pay heed to instructions.)

This contriver was Stephen's new saint: a saint whose miracles were explicable. Mathematics, aerodynamics, such codified lore, arcane to the impatient, might supply in modern times the efficacy of that moment when the orthodox saint invokes God, and is levitated. This means that if Dedalus is the artist's patron, art is no miracle but an intricate craft, the issue of which may seem miraculous. James Joyce commenced *A Portrait of the Artist as a Young Man* in 1904, the year after two Americans, sons of a bishop of the Church of the United Brethren in Christ, had flown on man-made wings at Kitty Hawk.

The Wrights' substantiation of an ancient symbol deserves to rank, in the domain of the imagination, with Schliemann's substantiation of ancient Troy. Their Dedalian deed on the North Carolina shore may be accounted the first American input into the great imaginative enterprise on which artists were to collaborate for half a century. Over its masterworks—*Ulysses*, *The Waste Land*, *The Cantos*, a hundred deeds of Picasso's, *Le Sacre du Printemps*, more—we may imagine inscribed that invocation to the Fabulous Artificer with which Joyce ended his *Portrait*. And the tag from Ovid that he placed at the head of that book—*Et ignotas animum dimittit in artes*—would have served a dozen other workers as accurately as it served Joyce himself. "Then he turned his mind to unknown arts": arts like those that had lifted brass and piano wire and sailcloth into the sky, with a prone man to steer the contraption.

Further American inputs were prompt to arrive. The movement was by tacit definition international, and no one worked in the country of his birth. Joyce (of Dublin) toiled in Trieste, in Zurich, in Paris; Ezra Pound (of Idaho and Pennsylvania) in London, Paris, Rapallo; T. S. Eliot (of St. Louis, Mo.) in Paris, Oxford, London; Picasso (the

Catalan) by the Seine. Painters dispensed with Newton's 3-D space; musicians worked with interdicted intervals; the poem, the novel folded time upon time, tongue upon tongue. Polyglot masterpieces were stress-tested, to validate new systems of connectedness, as that the reader's mind can jump aligned gaps, or that no uttering voice need be specified, nor unified. (Who asks, who answers in grave polysyllables, the questions in the seventeenth section of *Ulysses*?)

Then for fifty-two slaughterous months a war convulsed Europe, and the flying machines grappled over France. In Zurich Joyce toiled on at *Ulysses*. Elsewhere young Americans like William Falkner or Faulkner were tinkering with the biplanes they hoped to fly, and learning that the reason you wore a silk scarf into combat was to ease the friction between your neck and your windbreaker collar; otherwise you might be mortally disinclined to keep looking left, right and behind. Other Americans, like Dr. Hemingway's boy from Oak Park, Ill., were driving ambulances and getting shot at. Or like Francis Scott Key Fitzgerald of St. Paul, Minn., they marched onto transports (he in an officer's uniform from Brooks Brothers) and either reached France to face death or, like him, marched off again, the Germans having sued for armistice by the time the American army had rendered its young volunteers fit to be slaughtered. Fitzgerald was later to end up in Paris anyhow, and so was the young Hemingway, Paris having become, when the dust settled, the holy city of the great Movement. Even Dublin's Joyce settled there.

Young Fitzgerald (born 1896) and young Hemingway (born 1899) belonged to the first apprentice generation: the first to come to consciousness of the written word amid intimations that something so arcane and massive was going on. So they were among the Movement's first inheritors. You inherited it by reading magazines, and Harriet Monroe's *Poetry* and Margaret Anderson's *Little Review* had been spreading its news fitfully in America since 1912 and 1917 respectively. *Poetry*—on the whole a magazine dull enough to command Chicago money—had printed "The Love Song of J. Alfred Prufrock" (a lost soul named for a St. Louis furniture wholesaler), also fragments of Pound's "Homage to Sextus Propertius," the fuss over which got Pound fired as Foreign Editor. *The Little Review* made a bold try at printing *Ulysses*, and managed twice to get itself suppressed. Americans older than Fitzgerald and Hemingway, yet unlike Eliot and Pound in not having taken the expatriate's vows, had also contributed to such magazines: William Carlos Williams, for one, a New Jersey physician who had been abroad a few times but seemed to write like an impassioned though grammatical hick, and Wallace Stevens, a New York attorney whose language could be as cosmopolite as the old *Yellow Book*'s though in all his long life he never got abroad at all (his principal move was merely to Hartford, Conn., where he became an insurance executive). And Bohemian doings were afoot in Manhattan, where an alert-faced young woman named Marianne Moore with her hair done up tight in a basketry of braids did not allow her proprieties to be breached at Village parties, and set typewritten words into grids of counted syllables as though tabulating specifications for a cuckoo clock. She called these artifacts "poems," not knowing (she said) what else to call them, and sent a couple to Ezra Pound in London. His reply asked where her work appeared. Her reply specified wryly that she did not "appear," which was correct apart from such organs as *Bruno's Weekly* and the *Bryn Mawr Lantern*. "Originally my work was refused by the *Atlantic Monthly* and other magazines and recently I have not offered it. . . ." Her heritage was both literary and technological. Her father's given names were John Milton, and he had suffered a nervous breakdown after the failure of his plans to manufacture a smokeless furnace.

It was in character for the *Atlantic Monthly* to refuse

Miss Moore, as surely as if she had employed some taboo word. (She would never have.) Ezra Pound as a young man had supposed that it would be an honor to be published there, and it had refused him too. For its seismograph was infallible, and detected early rumblings of something not genteel: in fact, of souls committed to obscure arts. *Et ignotas animos dimittunt in artes*: writers were grouping under the banner of Dedalus, to practice art as though its moral commitments were like technology's. In the eyes of the *Atlantic*, they might have been arranging for queens to couple with bulls. For America, long permissive about technology, senses that art, if its premises be tinkered with, instigates red ruin and the breaking up of laws. No one takes art more seriously than a censor, which is what an unresponsive editor can resemble.

There was something, to American tastes, indisputably *foreign* about these arts, which seemed not to take art's obligations seriously, no more than did Dayton bicycle mechanics. Cubism was as much against nature as the flying machine—more so, since the latter "worked"—and had best be resisted though the flying machine might come in handy for wars. Even in foreign London, in 1910, one spectator of the visual avant-garde had lapsed into such hysterical laughter he had to be taken outside the gallery and walked. That was dangerous. As for literature, Pound's "Propertius" represented the Latin *tacta*, applied to young ladies, as the opposite to *intacta*, i.e. as "devirginated," a word which Professor W. G. Hale of the University of Chicago (Classics) singled out in a letter to the editress of *Poetry* as "peculiarly unpleasant." And in Joyce's new novel, it was freely rumored, a character visited the privy and (in a passage no one knew that Pound, of all people, had tried to soften in ms.) discharged his business there.

So appeared, to a people who were also putting up with Prohibition, the outlandish arts that threatened the Republic. Such were the canons the Hemingways and the

Fitzgeralds inherited. What happened next is instructive. America went on getting from the writers it rewarded what it thought it wanted from writers. It also got, want it or not, its own modernism, a homemade variety.

How that came about presents, after fifty years, the look of a movement, but the look is deceptive since the novelists and the poets were pursuing rather different ends. Whatever their later disagreements, whatever their pervasive misunderstandings of one another, Joyce and Pound, say, were engaged on a common enterprise. We cannot say the same of Williams and Scott Fitzgerald, or of Stevens and Hemingway. The novelists were courting readers, and homeland readers at that (Joyce's readers were not Irish). The poets were courting no one, and were hardly read.

In Rutherford, in Hartford, in Brooklyn, three poets who belonged to the Pound generation—Williams, Stevens, Miss Moore—persisted in their difficult craft as though writing for one another. A poetic was hammered out, as American as the Kitty Hawk plane, not really in the debt of the international example, austere and astringent. That was partly because, as if on some frontier, they could afford to disregard ways of being misunderstood. One way in which Williams' *Spring and All* (1923) differs from Eliot's *The Waste Land* (1922) is that Williams seems to be writing as for a time capsule. "A word is a word most when it is separated out by science, treated with acid to remove the smudges, washed, dried, and placed right side up on a clean surface." Later the artifacts that went to the moon were sterilized like that. His readers' expectations of "poetry" are not part of Williams' poetic as they were of Eliot's. And the folk who accost Stevens' player on the blue guitar—

> They said, "*You have a blue guitar,*
> *You do not play things as they are*"

—seem venturing to open a relatively cool discussion. Theirs is not the rage of Caliban at not seeing his own face in the mirror, which in Oscar Wilde's phrase summed up the usual response to the non-mimetic. Stevens did not have to confront that rage. It is intelligible that no Dedalian defiance, no prayer to be stood in good stead by a mythic protector, rises from the American poetic enterprise. The poets might have prayed for a large readership, but they had the good sense not to.

Fitzgerald and Hemingway, on the other hand, wrote bestsellers and made money. (This is not to say that their careers are parallel. Writing bestsellers—later, *enlightened* bestsellers—was what Fitzgerald had wanted to do from the first, whereas Hemingway had started from a craftsman's mystique and did not object at all when he found himself a bestseller anyway.) The scandal that attended modernity they assimilated and throve on. They received their rewards for bringing America news of a riotous generation, under everyone's nose but reputedly "lost," and also for impersonating its riotousness. Later Fitzgerald could be praised for a craft like Conrad's, and Hemingway for writing nearly as well as Hemingway, but neither man's art has been easy to extricate from his years as a public performer. Faulkner came very late to publicity, and was accorded it, when it came, on similarly extra-professional grounds: as owner and operator of a scandalous region, said to have a counterpart in Mississippi and pullulating with Snopeses and miscegenators. He seems artless and has not been thought much of as a craftsman. It is hardly remembered that he commenced writing, and developed the craft we may judge he never quite learned, under the difficult sign of Mallarmé (also, to be sure, with a head full of *Ulysses*).

So the poets, aloof from readers, and the novelists, surrounded by them, seem at cross-purposes. And yet they do hang together, the American Modernists. They shared hidden sources of craftsmanship, hidden incentives to rewrite a page, which we can trace to a doctrine of perception—the word valued both in itself and in its power to denote—very evident when we watch a second generation of poets (Oppen, Zukofsky) work out themes that seem shared by both Hemingway and Williams. That doctrine of perception, like general semantics, seems peculiarly adapted to the American weather, which fact helps explain why, from Pound's early days until now, modern poetry in whatever country has borne so unmistakably American an impress.

So writers of three overlapping generations, Williams' of the 1880's, Faulkner's of the 1890's, Zukofsky's of the 1900's, rethought and altered, perhaps permanently, the novel and especially the poem. Yet the homemade world of American Modernism terminates not in climactic masterworks but in an "age of transition"—we live in it—where the very question gets raised, what the written word may be good for. That question, we shall be gathering, impended all along, and one reason to retrace the making of the homemade world is to learn that today's disorienting view is the view of its skies, its fauna and its sun. Language—it was Whorf, the American linguist, who formulated this—confines what we can perceive, what think, what discuss. A fifty-year reshaping of the American language is the topic of this book.

It is neither a survey nor an honor roll. There are distinguished bodies of achievement—Robert Lowell's, Robert Frost's—through which the vectors it traces do not pass. There are representative careers—Hart Crane's, Thomas Wolfe's—that point capital morals but have less pertinence than the oft-told Fitzgerald story. And Cummings, the supremely experimental, trifler with the sacred upper-case font, dissociator of Aesop's very grasshopper into the hopping letters of its busy name? Yes, the book's theme is tangential to what interested Cummings, but does not encompass him because Cummings finally altered no verbal environment except his own. What the book leaves out should help underline the pertinence of what it includes. Permit that principle, and we shall get on very well.

A Homemade World

I ⁄ So Here It Is at Last

"So here it is at last, the distinguished thing," thought Henry James as he commenced to die; the process took nearly three months. He died on February 28, 1916. His ashes were returned to America.

In his last years, unnoticed by him as far as one can tell, an American Renaissance had been stirring. He would hardly have recognized it for a Renaissance: it was an affair, for instance, of a monthly magazine in Chicago (Chicago!) publishing little poems. A compatriot of his, a red-bearded young man with what he surely thought a facetious name, Ezra (imagine a Henry James character named Ezra), had undertaken to get "a few words of approval" from the exiled Master for this Chicago enterprise, "to quell the facetious East"—Boston, New York—where they thought it capital fun that any good thing should presume to come out of Chicago. "He is supposed to hate poetry," wrote Ezra to the Chicago editress, Miss Harriet Monroe, "so it may be difficult to elicit them." Difficult indeed; an effort by Ezra Pound to elicit the few words would have been a scene for Max Beerbohm to imagine. "I must bide my time, but I'll do what I can with him." There is no telling whether the envisaged confrontation ever occurred, or if it did, by what marvels of circumlocution James declined. He would have sensed that he was being asked to compose an advertisement. He and Ezra Pound (of the green trousers, of the single earring) had met a few times under hospitable roofs; Mr. Pound had been seeing the daughter of Olivia Shakespear, who was herself by way of being a lady novelist, and whose circles overlapped circles in which James moved. But a testimonial, and for a Magazine of Verse, and from a man old enough to have rebuked Walt Whitman . . . !

In 1910 Ezra Pound had returned to America, hoping to pick up some money, and earned there just enough for the boat fare back to England. He had also come down with yellow jaundice, which tended to infect his memories of that aborted stay in his homeland. But in New York he had noticed hopeful signs: the surging crowd on Seventh Avenue, "a crowd pagan as ever Imperial Rome was, eager, careless, with an animal vigour unlike that of any European crowd that I have ever looked at. There is none of the melancholy, the sullenness, the unhealth of the London mass. . . ." (In 1921 another American, sensitized by the same contrast, was to remark how a crowd moved in London: "each man fixed his eyes before his feet.") And architectural gestures: the Pennsylvania Station and the Metropolitan Life tower, which latter "dominates New York as the older towers dominate hill towns of Tuscany. . . . No man with sensibilities can pass the base of it without some savour of pride and some thought beyond the moment." He understood that this beautiful white building existed because a technical innovation, the advance of steel construction, had made it possible "to build in the proportions of the campanile something large enough to serve as an office building"; whereas there had been for some centuries no point whatever in building campaniles proper. "When towns ceased to need watch towers the 'campanile' ceased as a living architectural mode." Around Philadelphia, where he grew up, rich men had no inkling of living architectural modes, and built fine homes like castles.

. . . A castle something like Hawarden, and one something like Blenheim, and a great manor house (Elizabethan), and many smaller affairs of divers sort, and a number of older estates with splendid interiors; and none of this is architecture, it is all very ornamental, but architecture consists in fitting a form to a purpose, and a place fit to hold a garrison for defence is of little use to a man with no acquaintance.

He did not add, though he might have, that some of the money congealed into useless stone came from selling dreams; George Horace Lorimer of *The Saturday Evening Post* built opulently thereabouts, and so did Cyrus Curtis of the *Ladies' Home Journal*. Lorimer on his way to the station of a morning used to take a short-cut through the Pounds' back yard, where Ezra's father, a mint assayer, hoed corn.

Ornamentation, at any rate, was one thing, architecture another; and architecture—"fitting a form to a purpose" with the aid of new technical means—would generate as if by chance its own mode of elegance. Thus after dark, when the scrubladies turned the lights on in the office buildings, New York was perhaps "the most beautiful city in the world."

It is then that the great buildings lose reality and take on their magical powers. They are immaterial; that is to say one sees but the lighted windows.

Squares after squares of flame, set and cut into the aether. Here is our poetry, for we have pulled down the stars to our will.

"And this is a Renaissance," for it resembled the vigorous uncertainties that accompanied the first stirrings of the

Renaissance in Italy; so in 1912 Mr. Pound, aged 26, declared his belief "in the imminence of an American Risorgimento."

But patience, patience; the distinguished thing was perhaps not quite at hand. The author of the first poem in the first issue of Miss Monroe's *Poetry* (September 1912) had not been looking at stars pulled down to American will, but backward to Keats and backward to the Lotus-Eaters of Tennyson. The poem is called "Poetry," and Arthur Davison Ficke is content that poetry shall be the master mariner's teddy-bear.

> *It is a little isle amid bleak seas—*
> *An isolate realm of garden, circled round*
> *By importunity of stress and sound,*
> *Devoid of empery to master these.*
> *At most, the memory of its streams and bees,*
> *Borne to the toiling mariner outward-bound,*
> *Recalls his soul to that delightful ground;*
> *But serves no beacon toward his destinies.*
>
> *It is a refuge from the stormy days,*
> *Breathing the peace of a remoter world*
> *Where beauty, like the musking dusk of even,*
> *Enfolds the spirit in its silver haze;*
> *While far away, with glittering banners furled,*
> *The west lights fade, and stars come out in heaven.*

Though expostulation about much of the verse she printed ran through Pound's correspondence with Miss Monroe like a strand of barbed wire, his normal habit was to avert his mind from its presence. By this means he continued, for several years, to think of the magazine that welcomed such stuff as a sign and an opportunity.

Henry James on the contrary, in America six years before Pound, found it impossible to avert his consternated gaze from just the phenomena in which Pound was to discern hope. In New York's new buildings James discerned the very principle of the city's energy, namely the fact that it didn't believe in itself. "It fails to succeed, even at a cost of millions, in persuading you that it does." So it tore down, built up, tore down again. To the crowds that were to impress the younger man with their reservoir of animal vigor, Henry James' imagination "might have responded more if there had been a slightly less settled inability to understand what every one, what any one, was really doing." His attention kept returning to those crowds, and worked itself up to a set-piece of excoriation:

. . . "The state of the streets" and the assault of the turbid air [is not Dante's mantle upon him?] seemed all one with the look, the tramp, the whole quality and *allure*, the consummate monotonous commonness, of the pushing male crowd, moving in its dense mass—with the confusion carried to chaos for any intelligence, any perception; a welter of objects and sounds in which relief, detachment, dignity, meaning, perished utterly and lost all rights. It appeared, the muddy medium, all one with every other element and note as well, all the signs of the heaped industrial battle-field, all the sounds and silences, grim, pushing, trudging silences too, of the universal will to move—to move, move, move, as an end in itself, an appetite at any price.

And as for the arts, at Harvard in 1904 James had sensed a depressing absence, that of what he took to be the Great Tradition, the tradition of James Russell Lowell. "The muses had fled"; and "in what produced form, for instance" —he interrogated the mute scene—"was now represented the love of letters of which he had been so distinguished an example?"

The literary future, as it happened, contained a Lowell still, female.

Her name was Amy. Already, on October 21, 1902, aged 28, she had suddenly sat down and "with infinite agitation" written her first poem. "It loosed a bolt in my brain," she was to recall, "and I found out where my true function lay." She meant by "bolt," it should perhaps be explained, something from Zeus, not something from a machine shop; control of diction was never her forte. And early in 1913 the January issue of the magazine from Chicago arrived at Sevenells in Brookline, Mass., and Amy Lowell underwent a second revelation: "Why, I too am an *Imagiste*."

She belonged by divine election, that meant, to a movement that consisted at the time of two Americans and a very young Englishman. One of the Americans was Ezra Pound. The other was Hilda, daughter to Professor Doolittle who taught astronomy in Pennsylvania. They were both in London, where at a tea table in the British Museum Ezra had made rapid revisions on a poem of Hilda's (who had been his first love an emotional lifetime—say eight years—before) and sent it off to Harriet Monroe in Chicago over the signature "H.D. Imagiste." He perceived in its cadences, we may say, something analogous to what he perceived in the new buildings of New York: a functional bareness in which lights gleamed, the more beautiful because it seemed not to be contriving beauties.

> *The hard sand breaks,*
> *And the grains of it*
> *Are clear as wine.*
>
> *Far off over the leagues of it,*
> *The wind,*
> *Playing on the wide shore,*
> *Piles little ridges,*
> *And the great waves*
> *Break over it. . . .*

Curiously, it presents the same conceit as the "Poetry" of Arthur Davison Ficke to which Miss Monroe in her first issue had given pride of place. It presents a shore, perhaps Poetry, certainly intrinsic with poetry, to which an exhausted mariner has come; but no "streams and bees" are there to lull him, no "musking dusk of even": only hard sand, bright crystalline particles. No hum was present, no mush. Perception, unit by unit, slid over perception. (This was later called "direct treatment of the 'thing' whether subjective or objective.") No unnecessary word. And the lines fell not into units dictated by some meter, but into speakable phrases. (This was later called composition "in the sequence of the musical phrase, not in sequence of a metronome.") The average incult eye turned away with the mutter, "Free verse," meaning by this that the poet was taking things easy. (Doesn't anybody *work* any more?) The average instructed eye perceived *vers libre*, which dates from the late phase of *Symbolisme*. The eye of Amy Lowell saw her destiny.

What followed was a comedy as if by James, always positing what, alas, we cannot posit, that James would have perceived any merit in *Imagisme*. Miss Lowell loaded on a steamship her chauffeur, her limousine and forty trunks, and proceeded at once to London, to inform the headquarters of the Movement that she had arrived. There she met Ezra and Hilda and the third member of the Movement, Richard Aldington; there she displayed her work, all in *vers libre*, some parts of it less upholstered with unnecessary words than others; and when Ezra Pound that summer mailed off to Alfred Kreymborg a compilation called *"Des Imagistes"* for publication in the first number of his periodical, *Glebe*, lo, a poem of Amy Lowell's was among them.

By the following year she had reflected that this was less than her due. There ought to be an annual anthology, and each poet ought to receive the same amount of space, and the poems ought to be selected by vote. She herself would sponsor the enterprise. She converted Richard Aldington and H.D., who was by then Mrs. Aldington, and for good measure wrote (September 15, 1914) to Harriet Monroe at *Poetry*, Chicago, to explain that *Poetry*'s Foreign Editor, Ezra Pound, did not work enough. His work, moreover, she said, "lacks the quality of soul, which, I am more and more fain to believe, no great work can ever be without." (Is one sign of soul the use of "fain" in a letter?) She speculated whether the tubercle bacillus had attacked his brain; and though "this is merely surmise," the fact remained "that where his work is concerned he is failing every day."

Pound had the lack of grace to go right on working, and from then until she died in 1925 anything he, in London, showed signs of understanding, Amy Lowell, in Brookline, Mass., was to offer evidence that she, a Lowell, understood far better. "In this poetry business," she wrote to an intimate friend, "there are rings of intrigue." In that spirit she set out to cosmopolitanize U.S. letters. When in 1915 Pound's *Cathay* appeared, fourteen delicate poems after Chinese originals, based on tutorial notes a disciple of Emerson's, Ernest Fenollosa, had taken from instructors in Tokyo, it was clearly incumbent on Miss Lowell to "knock a hole" in them. She was soon allied with someone born in China: not, alas, a Chinese, but an old acquaintance named Florence Wheelock Ayscough, who at any rate was not Japanese and could address her cook in Shanghai pidgin. They proposed to stun the readers of *Poetry* with versions of eleven poems, done *correctly*, and backed up by an essay signed by Florence which should discomfit Ezra Pound and any residual adherents by explaining for the first time how Chinese poetry really worked, as disclosed to Amy by sudden intuition.

Harriet Monroe seemed not much interested in the theory of Chinese translation, but she did find the lines that were sent her rather cut up. Amy, taking a high hand ("It is always well to take a high hand with Harriet"), affirmed that she had made "an awful study of cadence." No such study, she claimed, "has been made by any other of the *vers libristes* writing in English. Even Ezra has felt and announced his convictions, rather than tabulated, measured and proved." Harriet did not offer to stand up against tabulation, measurement and proof. The translations duly appeared in the February 1919 issue, complete with Florence Ayscough's mild essay. "I am sick," ran one of the poems,

Sick with all the illnesses there are.
I can bear this cold no longer,
And a great pity for my whole past life
Fills my mind.

Awful, indeed, had been the study of cadence. Awful, next, were the labors to which Amy drove her poor fluttering lady Sinologist, who back in China was constrained to hunt out a teacher who seemed never to tell her what Amy wanted to hear. ("I explained," wrote Amy, paraphrasing a letter to Harriet Monroe, "that in getting you she was getting the *ne plus ultra* of Chinese knowledge and understanding; it being assumed, of course [though not by me expressed], that in getting me she was finding the best Englisher there was going.") Keeping up her end of their three years' correspondence, the *ne plus ultra* of Chinese understanding went nearly from nervous breakdown to nervous breakdown, sustained by the vehemence of Amy's will, and in their eventual book, *Fir-Flower Tablets*, "the best Englisher there was going" offered, as equivalent for the great Li Po, this:

. . . *I bid good-bye to my devoted friend—Oh-h-h-h-h—now he*
leaves me
When will he come again? Oh-h-h-h-h—When will he
return to me
I hope for my dear friend the utmost peace. . . .

The book was acclaimed, and Amy lectured on Chinese poetry before large audiences agog at culture. Amy's biography was later more than once written. She is part of a time's story.

The whole ludicrous tale illustrates certain principles, all derivable from the fact that literature today irrefutably contains Ezra Pound, whereas not even American literature any longer contains Amy Lowell. Pound had genius, Amy had mild talents; but setting, so far as possible, this huge disparity to one side, we may reflect, first of all, that the place from which to cosmopolitanize American letters was a cosmopolis, whereas Brookline, Mass., like Chicago or like Rutherford, N.J., was a place in which to perfect some affirmation of the local. Homemade cosmopolitanism has a homemade air, and Miss Lowell's poems resemble the effort of some Peoria craftsman to confect a *palazzo*. Miss Lowell did an injustice to her talents, and turned herself into a poetic Chautauqua. Dr. William Carlos Williams in Rutherford had noted before 1912 that

> *The coroner's merry little children*
> *Have such twinkling brown eyes,*

which was a Rutherford perception, and while he went on awkwardly to rhyme "eyes" with "no wise" and half-rhyme "gay men" with "children," he had fixed upon the kind of nucleus out of which, with some decades' work, a poetic of the local would emerge.

Second, it is characteristic of American genius that the casual eye does not easily distinguish it from charlatanry. Ezra Pound has stood accused of fake erudition; of wanton misunderstanding of such matters as Chinese poetics; of imposing values by the sheerest assertion. All these misdeeds are more pertinently illustrated by Miss Lowell's dealings with those *Fir-Flower Tablets*, from which, and from the correspondence about which, we may learn that her cynicism ("In this poetry business there are rings of intrigue") is the determinant that distinguishes these two poets. Pound knew less than he wanted to, and often, through impetuosity, less than he thought he did; Pound imposed by the sheer authority of his manner; Pound had better not be one's mentor, beyond appeal, on questions of scholarly fact. But he believed, with purity of heart, in what he was doing; whereas Miss Lowell settled for getting by, with whatever show of expertise would suffice to placate the natives. Purity of intention lies at the center of American achievement; it will cover, as in perhaps no other national literature, a multitude of lapses. Edgar Allan Poe too was a half-ignorant man who cared, and the fruit of his caring, to history's perennial astonishment, was one of the most arcane, most austere aesthetic revolutions in the history of a far more sophisticated country than his America. Stéphane Mallarmé even learned English to read "Ulalume" and "The Raven" in the original, and read there what Poe's hobbled technique had not allowed him to put there. Modern American writing is about honesty; we shall find that Scott Fitzgerald's complex presentation of Jay Gatsby, *né* Jimmy Gatz, affords a paradigm.

Third, American literature is tricky for the critic. At the same time it exacts his services. Along with their work, its writers invent the criteria by which we must understand them. That is why so much critical writing, some of it good, has been generated around American literature, as though evoked by the novels and poems themselves. Even so apparently simple a writer as Hemingway has attracted a long critical bibliography. He invented a new kind of fiction; it is chiefly in this respect that he resembles a Wallace Stevens, a William Carlos Williams, a Marianne Moore, who resemble one another in having invented new kinds of poems. So the creator's responsibility is severe, and discharging it may require a fairly long life. Keats was Keats by 24; Hart Crane by the same age was only beginning to be Hart Crane, whom, it is arguable, he did not live to become. Williams became Williams only at 40; in the great deal he had written before *Spring and All* we discover a few interesting anthology pieces. Pound wrote the *Pisan Cantos* at 60, after a longer life than James Joyce had, and his earlier work stood revealed.

And what are we to make of the inert public that keeps Amy Lowell's *Collected Poems* in print? Her book has become a *lar* to go behind the glass doors of a culture altar, side by side with other "best-loved" literary artifacts, the *lares* of 'gentility. Lord, Lord, all those unread, unreadable books: by Stephen Vincent Benét and the other Benét, and Elinor Wylie and what's her name, the candle woman, Miss Millay, Edna St. Vincent; and there was Booth Tarkington once, whom Scott Fitzgerald admired, and James Branch Cabell, whose *Jurgen* was fine writing, and John Erskine, who wrote of Helen, her private life; and Louis Untermeyer made anthologies once, and Vachel Lindsay was admired, whose manner was so formulaic that Pound once parodied it at the rate of twenty-nine lines in "one minute 58 seconds by the clock"—

> *O the prancing pig in the great big box*
> *Gave seven squeaks and the gilded cocks*
> *Crowed for the morning light,*
> *So bright,*
> *By gosh!*
> *The hash*
> *Is ready in the bright blue platter,*
> *And the farm hands' knives make a chattering clatter . . .*

—with a guarantee "to keep it up at the same rate eight hours per day as long as the demand holds out." Though the demand for new Lindsay was never cogent, his *Poems* were to enter the convention of the "best-loved." Best-loved, best-loved: *où sont les bien-aimés d'antan*?

At the Bookshop, among the greeting cards and the floral wrapping-paper: for presentation to convalescents judged as deserving of more than the latest Joan Walsh Anglund. All these temperaments were clever and sensitive once; all sooner or later, and many alarmingly sooner, made their peace with gentility. Their bones have not lasted.

The real thing, by contrast, has tended to be somewhat disreputable. In the thirties one read Hemingway and Dos Passos and Pound in *Esquire*, a journal whose proportion to normal journals, in format as in price, was as that of a call-house to a commercial hotel. Nor was it by any means the best work of those authors that one read there. *Esquire* paid them to be chattily male, cashing in on their reputation for putting their feet on the furniture. Fitzgerald, in the twenties, seemed naughty, and Hemingway brutal; both acquired a commercial publisher, Scribner's, which found these qualities marketable, though Charles Scribner, Jr., who thought Fitzgerald's first novel neither dignified nor beyond reproach and for whom Hemingway crackled with obscenity, at first took on both authors only at the insistence of an editor, Maxwell Perkins, who actually discerned and believed in talent. Hemingway came to Perkins and Scribner's from Horace Liveright, who is a better index than Max Perkins to the publishing climate of the times. Though seven of the authors Liveright published in a six-year span were to win Nobel prizes eventually, though Liveright issued *The Waste Land* without pretending to understand it, though Pound's *Personae* was a book of his, and Cummings' *The Enormous Room* and Hart Crane's *The Bridge* (not to mention *An American Tragedy* and the plays of Eugene O'Neill), Liveright's most visible energies went into such projects as arranging a nudist-camp safari for all the literary editors in New York to promote a book on nudism, or cashing in on the dirty bits of Petronius by marketing at thirty dollars a limited edition of the *Satyricon*, piously priced too high for juveniles, and intended, he said, for collectors, scholars and "other mature and incorruptible persons": defined in practice as persons who had $30. His specialty was lucrative trash, and he early discovered the immense advertising value of the censors. Something called *Replenishing Jessica* sold 33,000 copies after its entire 272 pages had been read aloud in a courtroom. (The reader was the New York State District Attorney. The jurors tended to fall asleep.) He made money out of Freud, who seemed to be saying that everything came down to sex. He made money out of *Flaming Youth*, which purported to be by a rebellious young sexist named "Warner Fabian" and was in fact the work of a middle-aged journalist inspired by the sales of *This Side of Paradise*. Before that he had made money out of Trotsky and out of John Reed's *Ten Days That Shook the World;* it was the collapse of the market for revolution that sent him toward polite pornography, as it had been the absence of any market for his Pick-Quick toilet paper that inspired him to join Alfred Boni in founding the Modern Library.

A market for revolution, a market for polite pornography, a market above all for continental authors: these markets, diligently exploited by Horace Liveright and others, epitomized the book buyer's suspicion that the likes of Houghton Mifflin were keeping something from him. Fruit, in the Prohibition years, was by definition something forbidden. The surest way to sell anything to anybody was to convince him that it was something the respectable didn't want him to have. How many copies of *Ulysses* were smuggled into the country there is no way of guessing: they came over the border from Canada like rum, or one by one in tourists' luggage, or in the keeping of a bribable first mate whom the London publisher's partner had located, or actually unbound and stripped into sections by a British wholesaler's workmen, and the sections mailed inside copies of the *Manchester Guardian* or the *Morning Post*, for assembly and rebinding on arrival. By late in the 1920's there was enough of a contraband market to make a pirated edition worth while. It was not proofread, since (1) the book was unreadable; (2) buyers were expected to snigger over it, not try to read it; (3) no buyer of obscene contraband would care to raise a voice in complaint, even if he could find anyone to complain to. It was, by bad luck, a copy of this piracy that Random House successfully sued the customs invigilators for in 1933, and many of its typographical errors were carefully reproduced in the first authorized American edition, as representing, apparently, avant-garde inscrutabilities.

Random House was the natural American publisher for the most famous banned book of the century; it had been founded on the purchase of the Modern Library from Liveright during one of Liveright's spells of financial stress, and the Modern Library list was from the first designed to suggest the fruits of a forbidden garden. Its earliest titles (1917) interact like phrases in a Symbolist poem to stir the book buyer's fancy and tickle at his will in the vague moment of decision when his hand hesitates amid books he has half heard of, or never heard of. They suggest glimpses into swirling depths: *The Picture of Dorian Gray*, and Strindberg's *Married*, and plays by Ibsen—*Ghosts*, *A Doll's House*, *An Enemy of the People*—and Schopenhauer's *Studies in Pessimism*, and a volume of De Maupassant archly entitled *Mademoiselle Fifi and Other Stories*, and *The Way of All Flesh*, and *Confessions of a Young Man*, and the novel of the atheist Hardy that commences with a bitter man selling his wife at auction. The series was an immense commercial success, with titles like *Treasure Island* and *Soldiers Three* to give reassurance that there were after all in these seas reefs of familiarity here and there.

Such, in those years, soon the speakeasy years, were the "classics": books that sounded a touch naughty, or that suggested strong stuff, stern and alien, of a different order from the connotations of Tarkington's *Penrod*. Their allure is hardly rational. The word *Married* in juxtaposition with the author's name, Strindberg, hints to the impressionable at a bitter vertigo. Had the author's name instead been Kathleen Norris, or Kate Douglas Wiggin, then *Married* would have given off ripples of bright triumph.

And books, the book buyer could not fail to understand, had radioactive potential, bone-eroding. John T. Sumner, standing with uplifted rod, cast a huge minatory shadow even over ninety-five-cent transactions, and his New York Society for the Suppression of Vice daily renewed its vow "to uphold our standards of decency more than ever before in the face of this foreign and imitation foreign invasion, rather than to make those things which are vicious and indecent so familiar as to become common and representative of American life and manners." A judge caught his 16-year-old daughter reading a book lewdly entitled *Women in Love*, and announced to the press his intention to prosecute all those responsible for its availability. "This book is a terrible thing," he said. "It is loathsome." There was never a time in America, probably, when more people, one way and another, took books so seriously, and in the process many books were read, and many more sold.

Foreignness: Europe: the threat and fascination of Europe hung over cautious minds like a menacing cloud. Conversely, to make cosmopolis anew, to make it here at home, this was the ambition of a generation of writers, some of them not even at home except psychically. Cosmopolis was Amy Lowell's *Six French Poets*, and the Poictesme of Cabell's imagination, and Hemingway's world of ritually tormented bulls, and the brave freedoms of *The Beautiful and Damned*, and likewise the quasi-automatic writing at which William Carlos Williams, M.D., spent some of his time:

. . . I'm new, says the great dynamo. I am progress. I make a word. Listen! UMMMMMMMMMMMMM—

Ummmmmmmmmmm—Turned into the wrong street at three A.M., lost in the fog, listening, searching,—Waaaa! said the baby. I'm new. A boy! A what? Boy. Shit, said the father of two other sons. Listen here. This is no place to talk that way. What a word to use. I'm new, said the sudden word.

Here we touch earth: it's an obstetrician's vignette. Williams always touched earth. Local earth grounds and locates his parodic *Great American Novel*, seventy-nine pages long. The ambition to write a novel that might earn that blurb was itself grounded, grounded in a sense of portentous vastness. Many had a shot at it. Even Gertrude Stein had a shot at it: *The Making of Americans*: massive: on and on: a great crumbling sandbank. Scott Fitzgerald had more than one shot at it. The idea that despite its social "thinness," amply complained of by James, America might be thought to exact from the writer something on the scale, say, of *War and Peace*, is less paradoxical when we consider the analogy of the great Russians, who are preoccupied by "Russia," as the American writer by "America," in a way no French novelist is preoccupied by "France." Physical vastness is a factor here, and also what James called a "complex fate," which was in part the fate of inheriting, each one isolated as though on a diagram, the problems Europe had spent a millennium evolving.

If the problems, the themes, had come from Europe, so might hints toward their aesthetic solution: for instance Joyce's deliberate structuring of a novel around a central myth. In November 1923 *The Dial* published the statement that the myth in Joyce was "simply a way of controlling, of ordering, of giving a shape and a significance to the immense panorama of futility and anarchy which is contemporary history." The author of that judgment, T. S. Eliot, betrays the bias of an exiled American; Joyce would not have described his material as futile or anarchic. "Instead of narrative method," Eliot went on, "we may now use the mythical method."

So here it was at last, the distinguished thing: an immense panorama of futility and anarchy, together with some hope of articulating it through myth. Scott Fitzgerald by 1924 was working from a pervasive local myth, vast as the continent: the myth of Promise. That myth was not home-made. It had helped propel the Renaissance. It was one of those foreign things, long naturalized, long reduced to the bare authority of a diagram. The bitter European books which the Society for the Suppression of Vice so disliked said that promise was deceit, and promise was American now. Even in Europe they thought so.

II⁄ The Promised Land

The Promised Land, America: so much so that in 1877, at Tingleff, near Flensberg, Germany, a tot was christened Hjalmar Horace Greeley Schacht. The name expressed his parents' faith that he would Rise, a process for which America afforded the world's paradigms. Hjalmar Horace rose to be president of the Reichsbank and "financial wizard" to *Reichskanzler* Hitler. Wherein his wizardry consisted is little understood, genuine though it plainly was. At Nuremberg he was acquitted of being a major war criminal, and at Lüneberg of being a minor or third-class Nazi. In 1970 he died quietly. Billions of Reichsmarks, affecting as they circulated millions of lives, danced through their double-entry minuet and vanished as his thoughts dictated. It was a career.

The laureate of the paradigms of ascent, of the way to move from obscurity to power as Horace Greeley had done and as Hjalmar H. G. Schacht would do, was a writer of some hundred books for boys, Horatio Alger, Jr. (1832–

1899), the most famous American writer since Harriet Beecher Stowe. The Alger Plot was simple and oft-repeated. One started meagerly; one shined shoes or sold papers and saved one's earnings; and one got on. Alger was clear that between honest industry and getting on there existed some Platonic connection, but he was never able to say what it was. Boys found it useless, therefore, to read one of his novels as a manual of self-help. If you scrutinized his plots closely, there was always a key no amount of honest industry could simulate: as when you turned out to be the long-lost grandchild of someone important, or as when, less implausibly, the child you pluckily saved from drowning was claimed by a man of affluence who called you "my brave boy," acknowledged that "but for your timely service I should now be plunged into an anguish which I cannot now think of without a shudder," and gave you a job in his countinghouse at ten dollars a week. Insofar as there was a practical formula it was this: that you should strive to be the kind of person who should deserve this sort of luck. But it was always, when you came down to it, luck.

And though "rags to riches" came to be the folk epitome of the Alger hero's career, like many folk summaries it was inexact. Alger did not typically see his boy through to riches, he merely saw him out of rags, driving a pen in a countinghouse, reading industriously, attending Sunday School, and plainly destined Upward. Yet riches, the tone implied, lay dead ahead; a satirist might have detected the smell of cooking. Alger's · definitive satirist, the director Preston Sturges, opened *Mad Wednesday* (filmed in the mid-1940's) with the final reel of *The Freshman* (1925). The rookie lineman, played by Harold Lloyd, saves the Big Game, entrances the millionaire alumnus, and is duly installed, pointed toward Success, in a countinghouse, beneath a photograph of President Coolidge. When the new footage commences nothing at all has changed except the photograph, which is now of President Truman. Harold remonstrates with his boss; he is not Getting Ahead. The boss concedes, in a fine set-piece of eloquence, that it would have been easy to start him at the top, easy but not American. The American way, he affirms, is to start at the bottom. Then comes the Decisive Event: Harold resolves to have a drink. The bartender, offered a crack at alcoholic virginity ("This brings out the artist in me"), concocts as though at Los Alamos a brew that will render his client *non compos* for hours and hours; and in a state of utterly stoned lucidity, incapable of remembering the simplest Algerian maxim, Harold zooms to the top in one day. (The process entails his somehow buying a circus, and later hanging far above city traffic from a leash attached to the collar of a lion that is promenading along a skyscraper cornice.)

No such surrealisms—perfectly plausible to a 1950 audience—presented themselves to Alger. For that matter, it was not clear to Alger what the affluent life would be like, though he had periods of comparative affluence himself. It was not even clear to him what adulthood would be like, except that it seemed not absolutely to entail there being two sexes. It was really not clear, in short, what one might aspire to, other than not being poor.

How to go about aspiring, that was what was clear. Frank Whitney explains the procedure to Ragged Dick: he must "work in the right way." What is the right way?

"You began in the right way when you determined never to steal, or do anything mean or dishonorable, however strongly tempted to do so. That will make people have confidence in you when they come to know you. But, in order to succeed well, you must manage to get as good an education as you can. Until you do, you cannot get a position in an office or counting-room, even to run errands."

"That's so," said Dick soberly. "I never thought how awful ignorant I was till now."

"That can be remedied with perseverance," said Frank. "A year will do a great deal for you."

"I'll go to work and see what I can do," said Dick, energetically.

So the recipe for aspiring. The rest will be luck, sure to befall provided you are so fortunate as to exist inside one of Alger's hundred novels. Alger died in 1899, a success story. Posthumous novels appeared for nearly a decade, some ghosted by the man who also created the Bobbsey Twins and Tom Swift.

On September 12, 1906, James Gatz, the 16-year-old son of "shiftless and unsuccessful farm people" in North Dakota, printed the word SCHEDULE on the flyleaf of a copy of *Hopalong Cassidy*, and beneath it,

Rise from bed	6.00	A.M.
Dumbbell exercises		
and wall-scaling	6.15–6.30	"
Study electricity, etc. . . .	7.15–8.15	"
Work	8.30–4.30	P.M.
Baseball and sports	4.30–5.00	"
Practice elocution,		
poise and how to attain it . .	5.00–6.00	"
Study needed inventions . . .	7.00–9.00	"

There were also GENERAL RESOLVES:

No wasting time at Shafters or [a name, indecipherable]
No more smokeing or chewing
Bath every other day
Read one improving book or magazine per week
Save $5.00 [crossed out] $3.00 per week
Be better to parents

Algerian character informs these resolutions, but they are not Algerian resolutions. "Study electricity, etc." indicates that Jimmy Gatz was aware of a principle that never penetrated the mind of Horatio Alger, despite his contemporaneity with Edison: the fact that mysterious forces could be mastered, and that one way to wealth lay in mastering them. (Alger's inventors are either crackpot or lucky.) And "Practice elocution, poise and how to attain it": Alger would have thought this more theatrical than moral, but Jimmy Gatz has somehow divined one component of "success," which is self-assurance: a different thing from being honorable so that people will "have confidence in you when they come to know you." Jimmy, moreover, by the time he is 17, has a new name ready for himself, Jay Gatsby, since Fame will not bless a Gatz.

Jimmy labors under certain disadvantages, being stuck in North Dakota far from the great city where so many Alger newsboys found themselves surrounded by opportunity. At 17 he has left home, but not headed for New York: it seems sufficient to be away from his shiftless folk and alone with his dreams, and he is bumming along the south shore of Lake Superior "as a clam-digger and a salmon-fisher or in any other capacity that brought him food and bed" when he sights a millionaire's yacht at anchor. This is the Alger Luck.

Alger would have called Jimmy corrupt. In the first place, he covets such a yacht ("that yacht represented all the beauty and glamour in the world"); Alger heroes are indifferent to such lusts. In the second place, he immediately puts into practice one principle of "poise and how to attain it": he smiles up at the yacht's owner, having "discovered that people liked him when he smiled." Alger heroes do not *use* their ingenuousness. He does do one Algerian thing; he does the yacht owner a service, telling him that "the most insidious flat on Lake Superior" is no place to anchor. It seems not to be his altruism that endears him to the millionaire, but his appearance of being "quick and extravagantly ambitious." Deep has called unto deep, and the millionaire in turn does an Algerian thing: he takes Jimmy to Duluth and buys him "a blue coat, six pairs of white duck trousers, and a yachting cap." Jimmy spends the next five years in the millionaire's business intimacy. Of the millions, $25,000 is willed to him. Thanks to legal chicanery, he never collects it. He has not even a job in a countinghouse. He has (in a world somewhat less unreal than Alger's) something more to the point: "his singularly appropriate education." Thanks to those five years, he knows how big business is done. That is why seven years later, after the war and after five months spent, thanks to an Army mistake, at Oxford (post-graduate work in "poise and how to attain it"), he knows how to be of use to his second benefactor, Meyer Wolfsheim.

Meyer Wolfsheim, who looks like a dentist and whose cuff buttons are made of human molars, would not have pleased Alger. "He's the man who fixed the World's Series back in 1919."

"How did he happen to do that?" I asked after a minute.
"He just saw the opportunity."
"Why isn't he in jail?"
"They can't get him, old sport. He's a smart man."

In 1919 Gatsby asked Meyer Wolfsheim for a job.

"He hadn't eat anything for a couple of days. 'Come on have some lunch with me,' I said. He ate more than four dollars' worth of food in half an hour."
"Did you start him in business?" I inquired.
"Start him! I made him."
"Oh."
"I raised him up out of nothing, right out of the gutter. I saw right away he was a fine-appearing, gentlemanly young man, and when he told me he was an Oggsford I knew I could use him good. I got him to join up in the American Legion and he used to stand high there. Right off he did some work for a client of mine up to Albany. We were so thick like that in everything"—he held up two bulbous fingers—"always together."

I wondered if this partnership had included the World's Series transaction in 1919.

By the late spring of 1922, despite these irregularities in the launching formula, the former Jimmy Gatz is on a trajectory millions of Alger readers could identify as extrapolated from the Alger novels. He is fabulously wealthy. By late summer of the same year he has been shot.

It is clear that Scott Fitzgerald, who created Gatsby, understood several things that Horatio Alger, Jr., never felt the need to consider, notably how vast wealth could most plausibly be amassed in a very short time, and how an ambitious youth should best prepare himself for benefactors who may put opportunity of that kind in his way. He had best cultivate Readiness, i.e. poise and how to attain it, and make use of such observations as that people like him when he smiles. He also needs a "Platonic conception of himself," which means the awareness that he deserves to be what he is not, and he needs a fierce determination to become that new self. Emma Bovary was similarly equipped, though more vaguely. Thus when Jimmy Gatz was 17,

. . . his heart was in a constant, turbulent riot. The most grotesque and fantastic conceits haunted him in his bed at night. A universe of ineffable gaudiness spun itself out in his brain while the clock ticked on the wash-stand and the moon soaked with wet light his tangled clothes upon the floor. Each night he added to the pattern of his fancies until drowsiness closed down upon some vivid scene with an oblivious embrace.

And when Jay Gatsby was 31 or 32,

. . . In his blue gardens men and girls came and went like moths among the whisperings and the champagne and the stars. At high tide in the afternoon I watched his guests diving from the tower of his raft, or taking the sun on the hot sand of his beach while his two motor-boats slit the waters of the

Sound, drawing aquaplanes over cataracts of foam. . . . And on Mondays eight servants, including an extra gardener, toiled all day with mops and scrubbing-brushes and hammers and garden-shears, repairing the ravages of the night before.

So an arc is completed, and the "universe of ineffable gaudiness" is made real, for what it is worth. To get it, Jimmy Gatz had first to conceive it. The first requisite is the Dream.

It has been dreamed since the Renaissance, and Gatsby is the last Renaissance Man. "Wait a little," was the Renaissance word, "wait while we settle these political distractions, and then watch." (Some impatient folk meanwhile crossed the Atlantic rather than wait about in England or Spain or Holland.) Late in the eighteenth century two long-deferred installments were delivered: merely a pair of revolutions. By the nineteenth century the fact at last grew evident that the Renaissance was no more going to pay off than the South Sea Bubble. In informal bankruptcy, it handed over, at two cents on the dollar, a few toys, a steam engine, a spinning jenny. So much for the promise to make us all as gods. (And entrepreneurs in steam and cotton suddenly began growing rich, and their managerial employees and their lawyers, and many of them mistook riches for the godlike state.) The state of being as gods eluded men, and yet it had been promised, and promised anew in schoolrooms, and Romanticism like Revolution promised it, and Horatio Alger, Jr. The promissory notes were everywhere. Fictions afford us glimpses of hapless souls, Bouvard and Pécuchet, Leopold Bloom, still trying to cash in, or rather the former trying, the latter simply hoping. And since the Renaissance dream has lived in each secular breast, an orgy of self-deprecation commences, each man confronting in his own way his bankruptcy. For contingency has encountered its own contingent status (not that anyone puts the situation that way). Emma Bovary destroys herself in what must be called false humility. Humility like so much else is in crisis, and no theologian, given the secular categories, can any longer define this now most elusive of the virtues. (One can even argue that it was Jay Gatsby's salient virtue: the pleasure he took in his house and his hydroplane and his shirts measured his sense of how far their lavishness exceeded his deserts.) Near the end, Sigmund Freud diagrams a civilization's rite of self-hatred: we are to tell Columbus and Michelangelo that we and they and all they bade us hope are nothing but the raging id and the despicable ego, beyond reclaim, and the fault happened in our childhood. By 1950, on the continent, Existentialism had no use for itself whatever, and the cardinal virtue, while one could keep it up, was Stoicism ("a philosophy for slaves," T. S. Eliot had written, redirecting Gibbon's shaft against Christianity). In 1961 Ernest Hemingway killed himself, everyone's Stoic. Emma Bovary, *c'est nous*.

But in 1925 it was still possible to recapture the Dream, or at least how it had felt to be one of the Renaissance voyagers who had dreamed it:

And as the moon rose higher the inessential houses began to melt away until gradually I became aware of the old island here that flowered once for Dutch sailors' eyes—a fresh, green breast of the new world. Its vanished trees, the trees that had made way for Gatsby's house, had once pandered in whispers to the last and greatest of all human dreams; for a transitory enchanted moment man must have held his breath in the presence of this continent, compelled into an esthetic contemplation he neither understood nor desired, face to face for the last time in history with something commensurate to his capacity for wonder.

This is almost a twentieth-century American *topos*, this effort to recapture the sensations of the early explorers. It haunts the imagination of the 1920's—as for instance in the Columbus chapter of William Carlos Williams' *In the*

American Grain—and recurs as late as 1942 in a work of history, Samuel Eliot Morison's *Admiral of the Ocean Sea*. There we read that mortal men may never again "hope to recapture the amazement, the wonder, the delight of those October days in 1492 when the New World gracefully yielded her virginity to the conquering Castilians."

But such feelings are ours, not theirs. The Castilians, far from marveling at a New World, were trying to identify features of an old one: the archipelago off Asia which Marco Polo had described. They were sure they were quite near Japan, and the next day they set off to look for it. Only gradually, and very reluctantly, as the experience of subsequent voyagers accumulated, was the faith that they had found Asia given up. To give it up meant not only to concede that the expeditions had failed of their explicit goal, it meant also to conceive that the great Earth Island, Eurasia-Africa, on which all men were clearly children of Adam, could no longer be what it had always been, the One World. If the Americas had not been inhabited, this would have posed less difficulty; but the strange land swarmed with men (were they really men? children of God? sharing in the Redemption, meriting baptism?).

Coming to terms with much inconvenient fact, the sixteenth-century imagination made the enormous effort of imagining that a second world, a New World, could exist, a process which Edmundo O'Gorman in a subtle book has aptly called "the Invention of America." America in that sense was one of the major feats of the Renaissance imagination; Fitzgerald was more right than he perhaps knew when he had the Dutch sailors who marveled at Long Island, some decades after America was securely invented, respond as though to whispered pandering, a pandering to "the last and greatest of all human dreams." Their response was not to trees and land simply *there*, but to a world audaciously imagined, a world man had found it in him to conceive. Even so, transcending mere North Dakota facts,

Jimmy Gatz had conceived Jay Gatsby, titanic, a transcension of the humble actualities that govern normal eating, talking, willing, coming, going.

He is the Renaissance magnifico:

He took out a pile of shirts and began throwing them, one by one, before us, shirts of sheer linen and thick silk and fine flannel, which lost their folds as they fell and covered the table in many-colored disarray. While we admired he brought more and the soft rich heap mounted higher—shirts with stripes and scrolls and plaids in coral and apple-green and lavender and faint orange, with monograms of Indian blue. Suddenly, with a strained sound, Daisy bent her head into the shirts and began to cry stormily.

"They're such beautiful shirts," she sobbed, her voice muffled in the thick folds. "It makes me sad because I've never seen such—such beautiful shirts before."

So much can be written only of his shirts. As to his valor, his hundred and thirty men with sixteen Lewis guns held off three German divisions for two days, and he holds the Orderi di Danilo from the Montenegran government. As to his experience of the world, he has been photographed, cricket bat in hand, at Oxford. As to his prodigality, we have glimpsed it, party on party. As to his way of getting from place to place, in the heyday of the Model T, here is his car:

It was a rich cream color, bright with nickel, swollen here and there in its monstrous length with triumphant hat-boxes and supper-boxes and tool-boxes, and terraced with a labyrinth of wind-shields that mirrored a dozen suns.

Where he passes, the very sun in the sky is multiplied. Two words, "swollen" and "monstrous," denote another man's resistance to what this young god offers: such resistance as we might feel did a monstrous angel abuse us by setting a huge pink foot down from a cloud. "An unbroken series of successful gestures"—that is one summary of Gatsby's style; and "something gorgeous about him, some heightened sensitivity to the promises of life"; and "an extraordinary gift for hope, a romantic readiness. . . ." Affluence, which can buy cars and underwrite parties, cannot confer those qualities; his capacity to imagine a style, punctured however often with whatever dismal absurdities, is what earns Gatsby the epithet "Great." An owl-eyed man who understands how wealth will normally manufacture appearances delivers what he means to be the ultimate encomium: the books in Gatsby's Gothic library are *real*. "Absolutely real— have pages and everything. I thought they'd be a nice durable cardboard. . . . It's a triumph. What thoroughness!" Invoking an American absolute, show-biz, he calls the Great One "a regular Belasco," and adds that he "knew when to stop, too—didn't cut the pages."

But Owl-eyes vulgarizes Gatsby, Owl-eyes for whom Belasco is the measure of all things (David Belasco, 1859–1931, dramatist and impresario, author of *The Girl of the Golden West*). Owl-eyes supposes that the intention of Gatsby was to create an effect. But Gatsby, save when he is being (understandably) misleading about his past, is innocent of the lust after effects. For life is infinite. Someday he may read those books, much as one night, having turned on all the lights in his house ("the whole corner of the peninsula was blazing with light"), he occupies himself with "glancing into some of the rooms."

So God saw that it was good. And, surpassing God, Gatsby imagines—has not even so much as thought it an audacious imagining—that innocent will can roll back the tide of events.

"I wouldn't ask too much of her," I ventured. "You can't repeat the past."

"Can't repeat the past?" he cried incredulously. "Why of course you can!"

He proposes to "fix everything just the way it was before." No Alger newsboy ever dreamed such things, nor did Alger.

What Alger dreamed of we are free to imagine. The author of *Alger: A Biography Without a Hero* tells us that his dream was to write a great novel. One day he arrived at the perfect title—*Tomorrow*—and the perfect theme, "a man who goes to the guillotine in place of his friend. The scene will be the French Revolution, and I have already begun to collect facts for the background." When it was pointed out that he was drawing on unconscious memories of *A Tale of Two Cities*, he "insisted that the title was still magnificent; he would simply think of some other plot to go with it."

The ambition to write, the biographer specifies, had been with Horatio since a diary entry of his late teens: "Am reading Moby Dick and find it exciting. What a thrilling life the literary must be! Imagination and observation —these I take to be the important requisites. Would it be desirable for me to take up writing as a life work? The satisfaction resulting from a beautiful story must be inspiring. . . . Have I the ability to write? Why not—if I am conscientious and observe closely all that goes on around me?"

Otherwise he did not know what he wanted of life, no more than did his newsboys. To be a writer, he thought he ought to make notes, especially abroad. In the biography this naïvete is plausible. His adventures abroad are chronicled. He visited Notre Dame, and made a note: "A big place and I didn't stay there long." He visited the Paris morgue, was seized on there by a *café chanteuse* named Elise, had difficulty making out what she wanted, entered her apartment at last, and wrote in his diary, "I was a fool to have waited so long. It is not so vile as I had thought"; but three days later, "Should I go on and is it right?" She introduced him to *la vie littéraire*. Then an Englishwoman took him in hand. He recrossed the Atlantic with her, but escaped at the New York docks on the pretext of buying a newspaper. Nearly thirty years later he was entangled again, with an entrepreneur's wife whom he had met through her sister. The reader of the biography may reflect on the difference entrepreneurs made to Alger newsboys. The sister made a difference to Horatio: her hysteria got him imprisoned a few hours on a murder charge. The entrepreneur's wife made a difference too. He and she, we are told, had a lengthy affair; he followed her to Europe; his mind, never very sure what was happening, collapsed. "The Great Idea, the idea that would make him immortal, began to take on what seemed to him a physical shape, dancing before his eyes. He tried to capture it, stumbling about his room." He was carried away kicking and screaming. There were more years, but no further adventures.

Such is the story we read in *Alger: A Biography Without a Hero*. It was published in 1928, in Harold Lloyd's heyday, three years after *Gatsby*. Forty-six years later its author, Willard Mayes, announced that when he wrote the book as a young journalist he invented virtually everything in it. Elise was his invention, and the note taken in Notre Dame, and the entrepreneur's wife and her hysterical sister, all the diary entries, even the Great Idea. He had meant it, he said, for a satire, but it got taken seriously. It boosted him toward success: he was to become editor of *Good Housekeeping*. There is something about Alger—perhaps something about Sincerity, for that matter—that turns fertile minds toward fraud.

When Horatio Alger died in 1899, Francis Scott Key Fitzgerald was nearly three years old. By the time Fitzgerald was old enough to form ambitions, it was easier to know what the ambition to write might entail. It entailed, for one thing, reading the kind of books you might like to write, with an eye to how they were done; for after Flaubert and

Henry James and Conrad it was clear to the most innocent that writing was "done," and in various specifiable ways.

("I knew at fifteen pretty much what I wanted to do," Ezra Pound recalled when he was 27. Have any people save Americans tended to conceive literary ambitions with such specificity? And "I resolved that at thirty I would know more about poetry than any man living.")

By 1918 Scott Fitzgerald (21) could say that a novel he was drafting showed "traces of Tarkington, Chesterton, Chambers, Wells, Benson (Robert Hugh), Rupert Brooke and includes Compton-Mackenzielike love affairs. . . ." (In the same year he noted that Bernard Shaw was 61, Wells 51, Chesterton 41, Shane Leslie 31, himself 21: "all the great authors of the world in arithmetical progression.")

He had natural gifts, sold a poem at 20, published a bestseller at 24 and another at 26, made money hand over fist from Lorimer's *Saturday Evening Post*, and in 1923 spent, he said, $36,000. He had also married Zelda Sayre, the headstrong belle of Montgomery, Ala. Along the way he had mastered several literary knacks, and derived some notions of how to put a narrative together, and vamped up some social and historical perspectives, and was ready to tackle a real novel, though he still had but one subject, Romance.

To list his array of devices so casually is not to underrate the expertise of *Gatsby*, but to note how inductively the expertise was acquired. He did not so much isolate and reflect upon techniques as observe himself responding to what he read, and sort out what had made for comfortable or uncomfortable reading. When after too many pages of preparation one novelist let something happen—a newborn's cry—Fitzgerald found this event without significance "except the strained one of making the reader think—'Well, after all that climb it must mean more than I think it does!'" That was his chief gift, fidelity to his own responses. Reading in this way, reading everything—*War and Peace*, well-machined junk—he remained quarter-educated (the American Tragi-Comedy inheres in his effort, at 40, to educate Sheilah Graham), but he learned how to set up situations and manage transitions without fuss.

He also learned how to get a frame around Romance, a necessary accomplishment since his model for Romance, like his model for the docile reader, was himself. Gatsby, he admitted, "started as one man I knew and then changed into myself," and was probably never very different from himself. Fitzgerald, for instance, shared with Jimmy Gatz a mystique of lists and schedules, and with Jay Gatsby sudden riches of which he was a little ashamed, and a passion for a lovely destructive woman, and the peccadillo of having invented Oxford ("I wrote *This Side of Paradise* without ever having been to Oxford," he remarked half in amazement).

In *This Side of Paradise* (1920) he had helped us look over the shoulder of Romance as it dons its glad rags:

> As he put in his studs he realized that he was enjoying life as he would probably never enjoy it again. Everything was hallowed by the haze of his own youth. He had arrived, abreast of the best in his generation at Princeton. He was in love and his love was returned. Turning on all the lights, he looked at himself in the mirror, trying to find in his own face the qualities that made him see clearer than the great crowd of people. . . .

This manner is bad enough. It could never be adapted to Gatsbyan dimensions without becoming preposterous. He discovered, perhaps in Conrad, the textbook solution, a skeptical narrator, whose use—this was a brilliant stroke—could be double. The narrator could grump about Gatsby's meretricious facets; meanwhile his temperamental resistance could slowly crumble, to calibrate Gatsby's magnitude. Hence Nick Carraway, who solves the book's major problem but is no exception to the usual trouble with narrators: his phlegmatic qualities, necessary to his function as strain-gauge, incapacitate him for writing the evocative prose that must nonetheless be written. Consequently when the splendid passages occur we tend to forget he exists. When he is letting us know he exists, on the other hand, he is sententious to a boring degree. "In my younger and more vulnerable years," commences the novel, and the reader, if Stendhal has trained him, winces. Within a half-page we are hearing of "the secret griefs of wild, unknown men," and so ersatz a locution as "the abortive sorrows and short-winded elations of men" is tendered us with the book not 600 words old. No one who can be so impressed by the cadence of his own wisdom as to use three such phrases in a page and a half is fit company for a reader of fiction. Fortunately Nick gets preoccupied with his story, and apart from his statement that he himself is "one of the few honest people that I have ever known," and his tight-lipped reflection on turning thirty ("Before me stretched the portentous, menacing road of a new decade"), he stays out of the way.

He remains an annoyance, the more so because his *sententiae*, which Fitzgerald no doubt thought impressive when he wrote them, ring so grotesquely we are apt to wonder if the author thought him important enough to caricature. For if so, then we see Gatsby in a distorting mirror of cunning design. Fortunately this train of thought need not be pursued. The author, who set out to be Nick Carraway, generally forgets to be anybody but Scott Fitzgerald, who could write the lyrical sentence about Gatsby's car, "terraced with a labyrinth of wind-shields that mirrored a dozen suns," and allow Nick Carraway to slip in but two words, "swollen" and "monstrous," among the enchanting forty. Nick is less a narrator than a conscience; though the less he says the better, the knowledge that he is somewhere around, like a saturnine big brother, helps keep Fitzgerald from talking nonsense.

—   —   —

As a "character" Nick won't wash. Though it has been suggested that he grows and learns, he seems not to do anything out of his growth and understanding but go back home, to round the book off, as mechanically as he came East to get it started. The accompanying reflections on East vs. Midwest give a spurious look of scale, but are beside the point and anyway evasive. Fitzgerald didn't need a geographical myth to lend import to Gatsby's story, and didn't really think he did; but artistic decency required a few terminal pages, which he filled with reflections, written in St. Raphael, France, about his 1921 return to St. Paul, Minn.

As a narrator, Nick has the deficiencies of the home-made. Henry James, more knowing, would have used him to locate a point of view without trying to pretend he wrote the book, and despite the technicalities of the first person, that is what he turns out to be: a point of view. He is a more useful one than Conrad's Marlow because he relates not merely Gatsby's goings-on but also a revision of his own response to them. That is his real use. As significant an event as the book contains is the shift in Nick's standpoint, reported as the last chapter commences with Gatsby lying dead: "I found myself on Gatsby's side, and alone." Since it is clear by this time that Gatsby lives by bootlegging, by betting rackets, by transactions in stolen bonds, a phlegmatic citizen is needed on his side to save the book from triviality. The glamour was meretricious; now the wealth is criminal. In short, the Poseur Exposed: too slight a plot for a second thought.

So it is important that the Poseur shall not have been Exposed: that a man hard to convince shall have been convinced of his worth, to balance the parasites who desert him, the thugs who prefer not to get involved, and the rigid hypocrite (Tom Buchanan) who would be crying "Ah ha!" much louder did messy terminal circumstances not compromise him. It is important, in short, that Gatsby shall be Great. It is important, because the central myth of the book has to do with Appearance made Real by sheer will: the oldest American theme of all.

Americans see things as they are: so they have always said. Nick Carraway goes out of his way to be "honest," though it is true that he has lived his life among Americans and is nevertheless one of the few honest people he has ever known. One honored President gained the sobriquet "Honest." The American girls of Henry James are honest, also forthright; Europe engulfs them in sham and pretense. But was Honest Abe honest? He was a politician. Honesty is a politician's role, particularly in a land that cherishes the story of the wooden nutmegs of Connecticut. Let Ezra Pound tell it:

> A man in Connecticut succeeded in manufacturing imitation nutmegs out of plain wood, and selling them at a profit. This trick sent the whole country into peals of laughter. The Centenary of this trick was commemorated at the St. Louis Exposition. Imitation nutmegs were made and sold at 5 cents each. One day, when these souvenirs were exhausted, the man in charge, a true son of Connecticut, pure-blooded yankee, did not hesitate one instant to substitute real nutmegs for them, at the same price. The public heard it, and roared again.

Then there were the Gold Brick artists, and the sellers of Brooklyn Bridge: folk heroes of a nation of metaphysicians, where nothing is more fascinating than the thing that proclaims what it is, and is very nearly what it is, but not quite. Or rather, one thing is perhaps more fascinating: the thing that is what it is. America devised, in California, a dramatic form based on photography, which, since the camera cannot lie, means that the actors are more real than real actors. America moved on to photojournalism, and latterly has devised the non-fiction novel, antithesis of the fictitious biography. It believes in a journalism that goes through the motions of telling just what happened. It was the last refuge, even after photography was current, of *trompe l'oeil* painting, a tradition that led to the *Time* covers of the 1940's, to enclose vivid fiction sold as journalism. Poems, even for American tastes, should be authentic; Dr. Williams seemed to avoid so much as a hint of metaphor. Pop Art came out of New York, its apotheosis the soup can that is not a studio artifact but a soup can, purchased in the supermarket and signed by Andy Warhol. Inside the American bubble at Expo '67 hung a 14-by-35-foot painting by Jim Dine, consisting of two panels painted brilliant cerise and flame pink, with the careful lettering,

These two panels have been painted with Sherwin-Williams speed print Sher-Will-Glo. The colors are brilliant cerise and flame pink. Jim Dine, Ithaca, N.Y. 1967.

One's instinct was to believe it. And in *Playboy* the month's *Maja Desnuda* has a name, a home town, a hobby, a set of breathless liberal opinions, and is photographed, not painted.

And yet, we know, we know. There are make-up men and press agents and skilled editors of verbiage and of film; and that famous President had little hand in writing that famous presidential speech; and photos are staged, and the TV men (we all believe it) create by their very presence the turbulences they document. No empirical test will suffice at all. Experts can be bought, evidence can be rigged, witnesses will clash in utter sincerity. Alger's "biographer" can invent diary entries. People who had never thought of believing what a politican said complained that a Texas politician-president was shouting across a Credibility Gap. Inside stories abound, by way of invalidating the Outside Story however plausibly its surfaces fit. And what is held to matter is intensity of intention. Gatsby is a bootlegger and a thief. What matters is the purity of his vision.

—   —   —

A kind of apotheosis of these principles is installed at the very heart of Fitzgerald's novel.

Once I wrote down on the empty spaces of a timetable the names of those who came to Gatsby's house that summer. It is an old timetable now, disintegrating at its folds, and headed "This schedule in effect July 5th, 1922." But I can still read the gray names, and they will give you a better impression than my generalities of those who accepted Gatsby's hospitality and paid him the subtle tribute of knowing nothing whatever about him.

Note, first, their subtle tribute; it consists in not asking. Note next the *trompe l'oeil* aesthetic of the paragraph: a genuine timetable, authenticated by its dateline, now "disintegrating at its folds," but filled, to authenticate this work of fiction, with names we are assured we will recognize; as we nearly persuade ourselves we do, though they are extraordinary names.

From East Egg, then, came the Chester Beckers and the Leeches, and a man named Bunsen, whom I knew at Yale, and Doctor Webster Civet, who was drowned last summer up in Maine. And the Hornbeams and the Willie Voltaires . . .

Note the effect of "whom I knew at Yale," and the effect of "who was drowned last summer"—the frank appeal to what we surely remember reading of—and the insidious plausibility of name after name, even, as we come to them, Clarence Endive and the Cheadles and the Fishguards and the Ripley Snells. (Real names *are* extraordinary; Gus Mozart sells Volkswagens a morning's drive from where this page you are reading was drafted.) And G. Earl Muldoon, further down, is "brother to that Muldoon who afterward strangled his wife." We have heard of him, surely? We seem to have. Dickens is behind this characterization by naming, and so is J. Alfred Prufrock, whose surname came from a St. Louis furniture house. ("You bring the girl," said the sign on a window full of bridal suites; "Prufrock does the rest." T. S. Eliot and the mother of William S. Burroughs, the eminent junkie, used to walk past that sign en route home from dancing class. Whoever can believe that—and it is true—understands how to go about according Fitzgerald the order of belief he is soliciting.) But Dickens' people live in a fabricated world, and Eliot's Prufrocks and Krumpackers in a world of the dream-grotesque. Fitzgerald is engaged in something subtler: he is weaving the grotesque so firmly into the real that their textures, however improbable the *Gestalt*, are thread by thread indistinguishable.

Gatsby himself is achieved in a similar manner; it is his very trash that grounds him in the real. His house one night is "lit from tower to cellar."

"Your place looks like the World's Fair," I said.

"Does it?" He turned his eyes toward it absently. "I have been glancing into some of the rooms. Let's go to Coney Island, old sport. In my car."

"In my car"—the crudely generous afterthought that does not think of condescending—is an even surer touch than the superb "glancing." Elsewhere greater risks are taken:

"After that I lived like a young rajah in all the capitals of Europe—Paris, Venice, Rome—collecting jewels, chiefly rubies, hunting big game, painting a little, things for myself only, and trying to forget something very sad that had happened to me long ago."

"Hunting big game" is too much; Fitzgerald knows it, and lets us know he knows it by making it the focus of Nick Carraway's unspoken scorn. But carefully though he revised, he didn't revise it out, nor did he delete, a few lines earlier, Gatsby's supposition that San Francisco is in the Middle West. He was not sure how far he might not have to go in establishing for the hasty reader of novels the fact that Gatsby is not quite what he seems to be. He even finds it necessary to have Nick say that listening to Gatsby talk "was like skimming hastily through a dozen magazines": and who knew better than F. Scott Fitzgerald what order of reality was contained in magazines? But even when the words are wrong the music is right; the cadence of "painting a little, things for myself only"—cuddling self-deprecation—or of "trying to forget something very sad that had happened to me long ago." That is the authentic music, the cello throb of *Collier's* and the *Post*, purveying with slick effrontery the dreams Horatio Alger could never quite realize to himself.

The magazine talk, and the obligation to devalue it, came from a psychic zone concerning which Fitzgerald could not but be somewhat evasive. Gatsby's grandeur, corresponding to magazine romance, and his falsity, betrayed by magazine rhetoric; his dream—to make so much money he could marry his lost love; his plan—to move the circus of his opulence next door to her and thereby win her heart; the symbol of his desire—a brilliant green light glimpsed by him night after night at the end of her dock; these are ingredients for a *Post* serial, with this difference, that in a *Post* serial it would not have been possible to contemplate her simply leaving her husband. (Nor, in fact, does it prove possible; the *Post* is ironically right.) And into Gatsby, the North Dakota parvenu with mysterious sources of wealth, went much that was pertinent to a Minnesota parvenu who had found he could write himself out of debt at will ($1,500 per story: $1,500 shreds sliced from his talent)—a knack denied to James Joyce and Joseph Conrad. Into Gatsby went much of his awe at his own Midas touch, and his knowledge of the complex bond that secured Zelda Sayre to him with hoops of gold, and guilt for his squandering of talent and material, squandering he was powerless to arrest because he was also powerless to manage money. "I don't know anyone," he wrote Max Perkins, "who has used up so much personal experience as I have at 27"; used up, he also said, on "trashy imaginings"; but the new book (*Gatsby*), he said in the same letter, would not be like that.

It was not; but it used those feelings; hence his realization (looking back on the first draft) that he hadn't known "what Gatsby looked like or was engaged in," his need to have Zelda (Zelda!) imagine Gatsby for him, drawing pictures "till her fingers ache," and his judgment, after the book was published, that Gatsby was "blurred and patchy": for "he started as one man I knew and then changed into myself." He even thought of letting Gatsby go and permitting Tom Buchanan to dominate the book; for Tom (the obdurate husband, the obstacle to a spun-candy dream) was the character unassimilable by *Post* fantasies.

Gatsby, his most remarkable creation, made Scott Fitzgerald uneasy, and no wonder. In the book he is—true—"blurred and patchy," but not always. Such lapses as obtrude from that spare prose we should barely discern amid the cadences and crescendos of a more opulent manner, for instance Conrad's. Considering how *exposed* is Fitzgerald's method, the feat he managed by diligent revision cannot cease to astonish: positing, as in the novel's epigraph, the romantic dream—

> *Then wear the gold hat, if that will move her;*
> *If you can bounce high, bounce for her too,*
> *Till she cry "Lover, gold-hatted, high-bouncing lover,*
> *I must have you!"*

—where the genius inheres in a definite article, "*the* gold hat"—and permitting us, without disaster, to behold the high-bouncing lover, in the moment that is to fulfill nearly five years' anticipation, "reclining against the mantelpiece in a strained counterfeit of perfect ease" and dislodging a clock with the back of his head; and remaining "Great."

How precarious was *Gatsby*'s success we may learn from *Tender is the Night*, conceived amid ambitions to achieve "something really NEW in form, idea, structure—the model for the age that Joyce and Stein are searching for, that

Conrad didn't find," and delivered after nine years' gestation into a world that didn't hail it as a masterpiece at all. Its numerous brilliances—passages better achieved than any single passage adducible in *Gatsby*—haven't obviated the consensus that something is seriously wrong with the first hundred pages or so. Fitzgerald was to toy with the notion that these pages, a long opening *in medias res*, belonged after all in chronological sequence, and years after his death the novel was even reissued in this disposition, but without real improvement.

He had been repeating a structure that had worked before, perhaps the surest sign of subconscious desperation. What we are shown in the first hundred pages or so (Book I) is like what we are shown in the first half of *Gatsby*: a man who will later come apart in disgrace, but now still dominating things, still in his glory. In Book II we are shown in flashback what the sixth and seventh chapters of *Gatsby* show us, partly in flashback: the stages by which this man ascended to his mysterious eminence, and also the beginnings of his decline (which his passion for a woman initiates). And the brief Book III, like the last twenty pages of *Gatsby*, forces us to watch while his life comes down in ruins. The arrangement of the two novels is so similar that we may wonder why that of the later one has attracted so much attention, as though Fitzgerald had attempted an experiment that didn't come off. But readers tend to be unaware of the similarity because they tend to be unaware of the structure of *The Great Gatsby* and much aware of that of *Tender Is the Night*, for the excellent reason that *Tender Is the Night* shifts like a broken bone after Book I, and becomes for the first time comfortable reading. This is because Book I is scattered, distracting, Fitzgerald being unable to do in Book I what he did so consummately in the first part of *Gatsby*: unable to enforce the magic, the consummate ease, by which his hero dominates the scene.

Gatsby dominates, effortlessly; that is the earlier book's triumph. Dick Diver does not; that is the later book's failure. So though Dick Diver's decline is harrowing, it is insufficiently established that he topples down from anything much: from anything save self-confidence and a career. And Fitzgerald didn't want a novel about a destroyed psychiatrist, he wanted a novel about the decline of the post-war West. He wanted, therefore, to open his longest novel— "the model for the age that Joyce and Stein are searching for": how that phrase rises up to plague his ghost!—with an apotheosis of the West's flawed dream: a blown-glass world of leisure and sensibility, united by tender filaments of *caring*, but so precariously united, so nearly on the point of disintegration into spinning systems of selfishness, that the caring (in this microcosm) is one man's only: the work of a magician agreeably ordering the tranquil days of thoughtless sun-browned children. As the Fishguards, Endives, Cheadles and Ripley Snells conglobed memorably at Gatsby's summer parties, and dissolved into semantic grotesquerie when Gatsby was dead and they were simply names jotted on a timetable, so the Abe Norths, the McKiscos, the Hoyts mother and daughter, and notably Mrs. Diver, the deranged Nicole, are held together by the spell of Dick Diver and scatter into their private egocentricities when Dick can no longer put forth that spell.

The spell of Dick Diver: that was the difficulty: the spell of a Gatsby without vulgarity, without the colored lights, the week's five crates of oranges, the Rolls-Royce, the speedboat, the orchestra: not garden parties like amusement parks, sponsored by a mystery man whom his guests don't know, but something that looks like a social organism: a reciprocation, a flowering, not showy, with at its center an accomplished man whose courtesy left "never any doubt at whom he was looking or talking—and this is a flattering attention, for who looks at us?"

In a general way, Fitzgerald understood the effect he

wanted Dick Diver to produce. Dick greets guests "with a proud bearing and an obvious deference to their infinite and unknown possibilities." To be included in his world for a while was "a remarkable experience. . . . He won everyone quickly with an exquisite consideration and a politeness that moved so fast and intuitively that it could be examined only in its effect. Then, without caution, lest the first bloom of the relation wither, he opened the gate to his amusing world." To an impressionable girl his villa—Villa Diana— seems "the center of the world," and we learn that the beach where we first encounter him and last take leave of him is a world he created "out of a pebble pile," lifting, shifting, raking. On it he performs, moving gravely about with a rake, "ostensibly removing gravel and meanwhile developing some remote esoteric burlesque held in suspension by his grave face. Its faintest ramification had become hilarious, until whatever he said released a burst of laughter." He is the Stylist, clearly, a life-stylist whom Fitzgerald modeled on his friend Gerald Murphy; he is also Scott Fitzgerald's effort to view from outside the fragility of his own charm, one of the things he saw mirrored in Murphy; and he is also a psychiatrist, blower of protective bubbles around patients who will stay tranquil so long as they are enchanted. ("So long as they subscribed to it completely, their happiness"—his guests' happiness, but likewise his central patient's happiness, his wife's—"was his preoccupation, but at the first flicker of doubt as to its all-inclusiveness he evaporated before their eyes, leaving little communicable memory of what he had said or done.")

These remarks, scattered through some twenty-five pages, constitute our sense of Dick Diver's spell. That spell Fitzgerald could talk about; the impressionable newcomer's shoulder (Rosemary Hoyt's) over which he talks is meant to distract us from the author's presence, talking. He could talk about it, but could not show it in action; could not show it, because it is coextensive with the novelist's wiles, the novelist's charm, the novelist's license to sweep and tidy his stretch of beach and make conversations agreeable. He meant to lay the spell before us, a doomed thing already rendered archaic by the war; he meant to show it sustaining a little world, and make that little world a metaphor for the great world sustained by money and by charm; he meant to bring the great world crashing down in 1929 (since Money underwrites it); he meant to write the Great American Novel. Like Horatio Alger, he could not quite imagine what such a novel would be like, because in fatal, fundamental ways he had never known his hero, his succession of heroes: Amory Blaine, Jay Gatsby *né* Gatz, Dick Diver.

He was already intuiting this lack when he acknowledged while *Gatsby* was in proof that he had actually not been able to imagine Gatsby (to write *Tender Is the Night* he would have to imagine Dick Diver), and later, after repairing the draft's worst lacunae, that he still "had no feeling about or knowledge of the emotional relations between Gatsby and Daisy from the time of their reunion to the catastrophe." This nescience, he perceived, he had "astutely concealed by the retrospect of Gatsby's past and by blankets of excellent prose," but it is precisely what the new novel tried to confront. Let the hero marry the girl; let him have what he wants; what then? For the twenties, he saw, was a time whose tone derived from people who had what they wanted. He put the book through mutation after mutation, carrying forward salvaged parts, till by 1932 he had reduced it to a story he could write: the story of Gatsby's (his own) marriage to Daisy (Zelda).

Zelda in her new role is called Nicole Warren. As Daisy, her voice had been memorably "full of money."

> That was the inexhaustible charm that rose and fell in it, the jingle of it, the cymbals' song of it. . . . High in a white palace the king's daughter, the golden girl. . . .

As Nicole, she was "the product of much ingenuity and

toil." (He had not gotten so far with Daisy as thinking of her as a "product.")

For her sake trains began their run at Chicago and traversed the round belly of the continent to California; chicle factories fumed and link belts grew link by link in factories; men mixed toothpaste in vats and drew mouthwash out of copper hogsheads; girls canned tomatoes quickly in August or worked rudely at the Five-and-Tens on Christmas Eve; half-breed Indians toiled on Brazilian coffee plantations and dreamers were muscled out of patent rights in new tractors—these were some of the people who gave a tithe to Nicole, and as the whole system swayed and thundered onward it lent a feverish bloom to such processes of hers as wholesale buying, like the flush of a fireman's face holding his post before a spreading blaze. She illustrated very simple principles, containing in herself her own doom, but illustrated them so accurately that there was grace in the procedure. . . .

All this had been equally true of Daisy, but in the earlier novel there had been no need to go into it. Daisy is spoiled and cruel, but this is not dwelt on. Gatsby is dwelt on, a symbol, not a man.

In the new book he also dwelt long on Dr. Diver, who was to be more than a symbol. In a working outline Fitzgerald called him "a spoiled priest." Despite the trappings of psychiatry, it wasn't really a psychiatrist he was imagining, but someone more portentous, someone who might be the clue to a world; but of course also himself. He may have been elaborating, in fact, youthful clerical fantasies that had haunted him ever since a wealthy, worldly and world-weary priest, Fr. Sigourney Webster Fay, a convert, had incarnated for his schoolboy mind some liaison between worldliness and unfathomable insight, and helped him believe, for a while, "that he would write the unwritten great Catholic novel . . . of the United States": perhaps a romantic apocalypse to parallel the *Lords of the World* of Msgr. Robert Hugh Benson (1871–1914), of which the last sentence runs, "Then this world passed, and the glory of it."

Literally, "passed"; but in a secular version the stock-market crash (imminent at the book's close) would have to do; that, and the wreck of Dr. Diver, whom Nicole and her folk discard like a squeezed orange, to have no more to say to a one-time denizen of his magic place than "You're all so dull," and to hear her reply with truth, "But we're all there is" (and, "All people want is to have a good time"), and finally to disappear into the practice of general medicine in the little towns of upstate New York, "almost certainly in this section of the country, in one town or another," pursuing at the memorable end of a botched novel the meager opportunities of the Promised Land, America.

III ⸝Something to Say

At fifteen, reporting how his brother "Buck" was spending a summer afternoon, Wallace Stevens wrote a letter like this:

At present he is on top of the house with his Rosalie, author of "Listigzaneticus or Who Stabbed the Cook," and while they together bask Buck's kaleidoscopic feelings have inspired the keen, splattering, tink-a-tink-tink-tink-tink-a-a-a that are gambling off the hackneyed strings of his quivering mandolin.

But at twenty, not long before graduating from Harvard, he was publishing in the *Advocate* verse like this:

> *Ah yes! beyond these barren walls*
> *Two hearts shall in a garden meet,*
> *And while the latest robin calls,*
> *Her lips to his shall be made sweet.*
>
> *And out above these gloomy tow'rs*
> *The full moon tenderly shall rise*
> *To cast its light upon the flow'rs*
> *And find him looking in her eyes.*

The 1895 letter (which also contains the words "beswel-tered," "fluctuations" and "scum-bedewed") points forward to the diction of *Harmonium* (where "A High-Toned Old Christian Woman" contains the words "citherns," "peri-style" and "squiggling" as well as the line "Such tink and tank and tunk-a-tunk-tunk"), but the 1900 poem points for-ward to absolutely nothing at all. He had gotten himself stuck headfirst in a perfectly empty poetic, the only one available, and it took the synergies of Austin Dobson, Ver-laine, Laforgue and Greenwich Village some fifteen years to get him out again. Dobson's is at best light verse—

> *Courtiers as butterflies bright,*
> *Beauties that Fragonard drew,*
> Talon-rouge, *falbala, queue*

—and the Verlaine of *Fêtes Galantes* and the Laforgue of dandified diction bare their hearts with the light versifier's wry smile, and Stevens distilled from them, with little inter-est in the bared heart, a species of nonsense verse fit to ac-commodate the most persistent of his lifelong pleasures, the adolescent's delight in queer words. Unlike T. S. Eliot, who learned different lessons from Laforgue, Wallace Stevens did not aspire toward specialties of feeling but toward a working grasp of what teased Lewis Carroll, the world-view a dictionary seems always nearly to enunciate.

American words are queer, and so are French ones. You can put one of each together: "beau caboose." Why not? "Catarrhs" (a very queer word, from Gk. *kata rhein*, to flow down; and has the English dictionary another -rrhs to display?*) rhymes with "guitars" (from Gk. *kithera*, via Sp. and Fr.); and if you write

> *Then from their poverty they rose,*
> *From dry catarrhs, and to guitars*
> *They flitted*
> *Through the palace walls,*

* "Myrrhs," as it happens.

you have, oddly enough, made sense, or so made it that the words make sense ("*laisser l'initiative aux mots*," said Mallarmé). And you can write, in a matching stanza,

> *The lacquered loges huddled there*
> *Mumbled zay-zay and a-zay, a-zay.*
> *The moonlight*
> *Fubbed the girandoles,*

forcing the reader, as he puts down his dictionary ("*Fub*, v.t., var. of fob, to trick" and "*Girandole*, n., an ornamental branched candleholder"), to reflect that sense can look strangely like nonsense when words do not look as if they meant what they do. It seems arbitrary that "fub" can mean "deceive," though perhaps no more so than that "cat" means *felis domestica*; as for "zay-zay and a-zay, a-zay," it designates mumbling no worse doubtless than "wang wang," in Chinese opinion, designates a dog barking. You can write a whole poem, heading it "Some Friends from Pascagoula" (which is, yes, an American place, in Mississippi), and call the friends Cotton and Sly, which are both names in any decent-sized telephone book, and invoke a conversation which may as well be of a bird's descent as anything:

> *Tell me more of the eagle, Cotton,*
> *And you, black Sly,*
> *Tell me how he descended*
> *Out of the morning sky.*
>
> *Describe with deepened voice*
> *And noble imagery*
> *His slowly-falling round*
> *Down to the fishy sea.*
>
> *Here was a sovereign sight,*
> *Fit for a kinky clan.*
> *Tell me again of the point*
> *At which the flight began,*

> *Say how his heavy wings,*
> *Spread on the sun-bronzed air,*
> *Turned tip and tip away,*
> *Down to the sand, the glare.*
>
> *Of the pine trees edging the sand,*
> *Dropping in sovereign rings*
> *Out of his fiery lair.*
> *Speak of the dazzling wings.*

—a sad poem, underneath, because no eagle swoops here, where you are, for instance in Hartford, Conn., and if an eagle's descent is to be recreated here (in Hartford) only the tricks of noble imagery and deepened voice will suffice. Yet, in commanding that these be adopted, you concede that they are tricks, as empty as would be any effort to tell ("again") of "the point / At which the flight began"—a point in the empty air: how tell of that? What a noble imposture is language. We may learn from Wallace Stevens, through its use, what occurs in the mental country of imagined friends from a Pascagoula identical only in name with the Pascagoula on the map of Mississippi; we shall never learn of the quiddities of Hartford. Words make a world of words. Local quiddities evade them.

A few years later Stevens explained to a friendly commentator that "Some Friends from Pascagoula" was "neither merely description nor symbolical." "Merely description" would pertain did the words derive their virtue from obedience to seen things. The words would be "symbolical" if the reality they call forth shadowed some remoter reality. No, Stevens said, the poem is precisely about the creation of the concepts it creates, and about a man's need for such a creation of concepts.

A man without existing conventions (beliefs, etc.) depends for ideas of a new and noble order on "noble imagery." This poem is an attempt to give a specimen of noble imagery in a commonplace occurrence. What seems to be mere description is, after all, a presentation of a "sovereign sight."

So the poem enacts the creation of a necessary fiction; and, Stevens had written decades before he was much heard of,

Poetry is the supreme fiction, madame.

In 1942 he wrote a long poem, "Notes Toward a Supreme Fiction," and walking home through a Hartford dusk discussed it with a student. "I said that I thought that we had reached a point at which we could no longer really believe in anything unless we recognized that it was a fiction." This is subtle doctrine, or homemade, as you will.

Anything words say is a fiction:

The houses are haunted
By white night-gowns

is a fiction, but no more so than "The cat sat on the mat"; and the statement about night-gowns has the advantage of being (in most moods) the more amusing. Also, not being bound to brute actualities, it implies a much larger universe of fiction.

Against which:

THE RED WHEELBARROW

so much depends
upon

a red wheel
barrow

glazed with rain
water

beside the white
chickens

—William Carlos Williams, 1923, not contriving a report from Pascagoula but obligated by the immediate actual. (At least we may think so, even if he remembered the scene, or imagined it, or saw it painted.) Two decades later, not long after Stevens excogitated his Fiction, Williams was writing—eighty miles away, and he might as well have been in Mozambique—that "A poem is a small (or large) machine made out of words." He went on to explain how the machine gets made:

> When a man makes a poem, makes it, mind you, he takes words as he finds them interrelated about him and composes them—without distortion which would mar their exact significances—into an intense expression of his perceptions and ardors that they may constitute a revelation in the speech that he uses.

The tail end of this sentence, as so often with Williams, slips away into rhetoric. But: "Words as he find them interrelated about him" —no hoo-hoo-hoo, no beau caboose, no fubbed girandoles—and "an intense expression of his perceptions and ardors"—so intense that rolled once across a reader's mind, it will leave its impress like a Babylonian seal. (Who has ever forgotten the red wheelbarrow?) So:

> It isn't what he *says* that counts as a work of art, it's what he makes, with such intensity of perception that it lives with an intrinsic movement of its own to verify its authenticity.

"Authenticity," that's a Williams word. But Stevens, 1946, having developed for forty years in a contrary direction, thought Williams' work empty:

> I have not read Paterson. I have the greatest respect for him, although there is the constant difficulty that he is more interested in the way of saying things than in what he has to say. The fact remains that we are always fundamentally interested in what a writer has to say. When we are sure of that, we pay attention to the way in which he says it, not often before.

This is one of the most extraordinary misunderstandings in literary history.

And yet it was nearly inevitable. Words, it seems naïvely clear, are to say things, just as a hole is to dig; and once we have set down words they can be considered under two aspects: (1) What is said; (2) How it is said. So if, for Williams, it isn't what the poet *says* that counts as a work of art, then (it follows by elimination) Williams must be interested in the way of saying. And this (Q.E.D.) is the lesser aspect of language. Any freshman can follow that, and Stevens among propositions had (as had Williams) the mentality of a freshman.

Yet if any poems have been simply confected from words, words shaggy, smooth, humdrum, exotic, words stroked and smoothed and jostled, words set grimacing, they would seem to be Stevens' poems; if anybody's syntax is what Donald Davie has called "syntax as music"—a Swedish drill in which "nothing is being lifted, transported, or set down, though the muscles tense, knot and relax as if it were"—the syntax of Wallace Stevens would seem to qualify. It is the perfect body of work from which to document a poetic of the pseudo-statement. But Stevens kept his simple faith in that division between (1) what is said, (2) how it is said, and no one can page through his *Letters* however casually without being struck by his confidence that his poems have paraphrasable content, worth the extracting. In the thirties, to Ronald Lane Latimer, and in the forties, to Hi Simons, he tirelessly explicated, explicated. "In 'A Fading of the Sun' the point is that, instead of crying for help to God or to one of the gods, we should look to ourselves for help. The exaltation of human nature should take the place of its abasement." In the twenty-ninth part of "Like Decorations in a Nigger Cemetery"—

> *Choke every ghost with acted violence,*
> *Stamp down the phosphorescent toes, tear off*
> *The spittling tissues tight across the bones.*
> *The heavy bells are tolling rowdy-dow.*

—we are not to be distracted by the Jacobean vehemence, nor by the diction ("spittling," "rowdy-dow") to such an extent that we miss What Is Said; for, "Paraphrased, this means: cast out the spirit that you have inherited for one of your own, for one based on reality." Stevens wanted the differences between ghosts and bells to enact this exchange: "Thus, the bells are not ghostly, nor do they make phosphorescent sounds, so to speak. They are heavy and 'are tolling rowdy-dow.' "

And because "we live in a world plainly plain" in which "everything is as you see it," Poetry—the Supreme Fiction —is "the only possible heaven." He never tired of saying *that*; on this occasion he was commenting on Part V of "The Man with the Blue Guitar," where the poem also says it, very plainly:

> . . . *Poetry*
>
> *Exceeding music must take the place*
> *Of empty heaven and its hymns. . . .*

So he had Something to Say, discursive variations on the familiar theme of a first-generation agnostic, and he was puzzled by "the universal acceptance of Bill Williams," who "rejects the idea that meaning has the slightest value and describes a poem as a structure of little blocks." If Williams' "mobile-like arrangement of lines" was what the present generation liked, what would there be for the next generation to like? "Pretty much the bare page, for that alone would be new."

Not what the poet *says*, insisted Williams; what he *makes*; and if ever we seem to catch him *saying* ("So much depends upon . . ."), well, he has cunningly not said *what* depends. He has levered that red wheelbarrow into a special zone of attention by sheer torque of insistence.

> *so much depends*
> *upon*
>
> *a red wheel*
> *barrow* . . .

Attention first encounters the word "upon," sitting all alone as though to remind us that "depends upon," come to think of it, is a rather queer phrase. Instead of tracing, as usage normally does, the contour of a forgotten Latin root, "depends upon" ignores the etymology of "depend" (*de* + *pendere* = to hang from). In the substantial world "upon" goes nicely with "wheelbarrow": *so much*, as it were, *piled upon*. In the idiomatic world, inexplicably, "upon" goes with "depends." In the poem, since we're paying unaccustomed attention, these two worlds are sutured, and "depends" lends its physical force, an incumbency as though felt by the muscles, to what must be a psychic depending.

(Here, to keep ourselves straight, let's borrow Eli Siegel's statement of the scope of this poem: "Williams is saying that if a curved useful thing, a wheelbarrow, can be red; and if the red can be glazed with rain water—that is, make a one with something different from red, something not of color; and if the oneness of a red wheelbarrow and rain can be attended by living things in white—the white chickens—the diversities of the world, seen boldly, can satisfy human life and a particular mind.")

En route to which, after "upon," there's what looks like a stanza break. What are these stanzas? Small change symmetrically counted, always three words and then one word; the one word, moreover, always of two syllables, but the three-word line having four syllables the first time and the last, but only three syllables on its two middle occurrences. These are stanzas you can't quite *hear*, especially as one very simple sentence runs through all four of them. They are stanzas to see, and the sight of them, as so often in Williams, inflects the speaking voice, the listening ear, with obligations difficult to specify. "Upon," "barrow," "water," "chickens," these words we punctuate with as it were a contraction of the shoulders, by way of doing the stanzas' presence some justice. And as we give "barrow" and "water" the emphasis their isolation requests, two other words, "wheel" and "rain," isolate likewise:

> ... *a red wheel*
> *barrow*
>
> *glazed with rain*
> *water* ..

"Wheelbarrow" and "rainwater," dissociated into their molecules, seem nearly kennings: not adjective plus noun but yoked nouns, as though new-linked. And "red" goes with "white," in a simple bright scheme, and "chickens" with "barrow" for an ideogram of the barnyard, comporting with the simplicities of rain; and the rain glazes a painted surface but (we are left to imagine) does not glaze the chickens, merely soaks them if they are chickens enough to stand in it. (And yet they need it, and may not be wise enough to know how much depends, for them, on the rain.) So much depends on all that pastoral order: food, and the opportunity to touch actualities (while trundling a wheelbarrow), and the Sabine diastole to counter the urban systole.

Are these reflections penumbral to the poem? Probably. Probably even external to it. This poem tends to ignore what it doesn't state. But let them serve to remind us that a farmer would know every one of the words in this little poem, but would be incapable of framing the poem, or even uttering its sentence. We need to be at a picturesque distance from such elements to think of how much depends (for us) on them.

"Mobile-like arrangement," said Wallace Stevens. Yes. The lines, the words, dangle in equidependency, attracting the attention, isolating it, so that the sentence in which they are arrayed comes to seem like a suspension system. This was one thing Williams meant by "making," not "saying." Yet you do say, you do go through the motions of saying.

But art lifts the saying out of the zone of things said. For try an experiment. Try to imagine an occasion for this sentence to be said:

So much depends upon a red wheelbarrow glazed with rainwater beside the white chickens.

Try it over, in any voice you like: it is impossible. It could only be the gush of an arty female on a tour of Farmer Brown's barnyard. And to go on with the dialogue? To whom might the sentence be spoken, for what purpose? Why, to elicit agreement, and a silent compliment for the speaker's "sensitivity." Not only is what the sentence says banal, if you heard someone say it you'd wince. But hammered on the typewriter into a *thing made*, and this without displacing a single word except typographically, the sixteen words exist in a different zone altogether, a zone remote from the world of sayers and sayings.

That zone is what Williams in the 1920's started calling "the Imagination." It is the place where mental clarities occur, for you no more experience clarities in your head than you experience vision in your eye. Where is the seen world? It is behind the eye, in a space you have learned to create. And where, likewise, is the clarified world (where "so much depends")? Ah, in the Imagination.

Which, Williams meant, is where poems are, in a space you must likewise learn to create. "There is a 'special' place which poems, as all works of art, must occupy, but it is quite definitely the same as that where bricks or colored threads are handled": are handled, of course, by the intending mind that can reach through the fingers. The poem that doesn't succeed in existing there is "the usual 'poem,' the commonplace opaque board covered with vain curlicues."

In that place Williams called the Imagination we may encounter such a flower as the rose from whose petal's edge

> *. . . a line starts*
> *that being of steel*
> *infinitely fine, infinitely*
> *rigid penetrates*
> *the Milky Way*
> *without contact . . .*

The mathematical happenings take place in the Imagination too—Pythagoras was at home there—and it is also where

> *the reddish*
> *purplish, forked, upstanding, twiggy*
> *stuff of bushes and small trees*

quicken in March. The poem called "Spring and All" seems to say that these quickenings and stirrings are "all along the road," but that road, being a road in a poem in the imagination, eludes all maps. It's the road "to the contagious hospital," another strange phrase, come to think of it (Williams poems often begin with slightly odd phrases). An Isolation Hospital, doubtless, a place for sufferers from contagious diseases; but "contagious hospital"? Has the place infected the land? The land does seem infected, a waste land, pervaded by "a cold wind."

> *Beyond, the*
> *waste of broad, muddy fields*
> *brown with dried weeds, standing and fallen*

—words written, it would seem, within weeks after *The Dial* published *The Waste Land*. In the little book where the poem was originally published it is preceded by a giddy manifesto against "THE TRADITIONALISTS OF PLAGIARISM," which would seem to mean, against such traditionalists as the author of *The Waste Land*, who put Shakespeare's "Those are pearls that were his eyes" into a poem he signed with his own name.

Williams' manifesto asserts that SPRING (his capitals) is approaching; that all is to be reborn (in the imagination).

(This does not mean an imaginary rebirth.) "Suddenly it is at an end. THE WORLD IS NEW." The reborn things

> ... enter the new world naked,
> cold, uncertain of all
> save that they enter. All about them
> the cold, familiar wind—

The "new world" they enter is the world of the Imagination, where

> Now, the grass, tomorrow
> The stiff curl of wildcarrot leaf
>
> One by one objects are defined—
> It quickens: clarity, outline of leaf

and

> rooted they
> grip down and begin to awaken

(and no terminal full stop).

For this poem, now so familiar, was once part of a book, and the book—*Spring and All* (1923)—was about the domain of the Imagination, where things are born a second time. There were twenty-seven poems in the book, of which the twenty-second was "The Red Wheelbarrow," then untitled. In intervals of eager talk about the Imagination, the book addressed itself to familiar topics like Poetry vs. Prose, and "The Red Wheelbarrow" may illustrate its dictum that poetry is not distinguished from prose by the presence of meter. "It is ridiculous to say that verse grades off into prose as the rhythm becomes less and less pronounced." For "verse is of such a nature that it may appear without metrical stress of any sort," and "prose may be strongly stressed"; in short, "meter has nothing to do with the question whatever."

The difference between poetry and prose is that poetry leaps into, helps define, that strange zone the Imagination. For—hold on now—"poetry feeds the imagination and prose the emotions, poetry liberates words from their emotional implications, prose confirms them in it."

This distinction seems derived from Williams' antipathy, beyond reason, to the sequence of words that draws such emotive force from the word "stony," the word "dead"—

> *What are the roots that clutch, what branches grow*
> *Out of this stony rubbish? Son of man*
> *You cannot say, or guess, for you know only*
> *A heap of broken images, where the sun beats*
> *And the dead tree gives no shelter . . .*

In contradicting this, he felt he was refuting an imposture. No: "rooted," he said,

> *rooted they*
> *grip down and begin to awaken.*

After all these years, how provincial we may think he seems, spitting against *The Waste Land*'s implacable wind. Yet there is one plane, Williams was alone in understanding, on which *The Waste Land* does ask to be agreed with or disagreed with. It implies a poetic. It offers to say—to show—how poetry must be written in our time. If nothing will grow in our stone civilization, if no dance is stepped to the sound of horns and motors, then the poet's recourse is to go back, to recover the old words, use again the old stones, learn the lost meanings: which means, for an American, rejoin the European past. His mention of April, for instance, will be poetry in remembering Chaucer's April—

> *Whan that Aprille with his showres soote*
> *The droghte of March hath perced to the roote . . .*

He may syncopate Chaucer's meter and embitter his sense—

> *April is the cruellest month, breeding*
> *Lilacs out of the dead land, mixing*
> *Memory and desire, stirring*
> *Dull roots with spring rain.*

But when he does this, and with a skill no one, not Williams certainly, is disposed to underrate, he achieves its persuasive eloquence at a cost: the fearful cost, Williams thought, of rejecting the New World's immediacies, the real language of men, audible in Rutherford. Not by what Williams on another occasion called "words hung with pleasing wraiths of former masteries," not by that means but by the transfer of today's actual idiom to the zone of the Imagination, was today's poetry feasible.

Round and round this topic he moved, making aphorisms. Words grip the solid world, but not as if describing it. "In description words adhere to certain objects, and have the effect on the sense of oysters, or barnacles." But not so in the Imagination, for "words occur in liberation by virtue of its processes." Nor does Imagination "imagine possession of that which is lost": it is not wish fulfillment. But do not run away either with the idea that words being liberated are liberated from sense, that they aspire to the condition of music, content with their attuned noises. (One might venture an example:

> The lacquered loges huddled there
> Mumbled zay-zay and a-zay, a-zay. . . .)

No, "according to my present theme the writer of imagination would attain closest to the conditions of music"— accepting that formulation of the ideal—"not when his words are dissociated from natural objects and specified meanings but when they are liberated from the usual quality of that meaning by transposition into another medium, the imagination." And "The word is not liberated, therefore able to communicate release from the fixities which destroy it until it is accurately tuned to the fact" (parenthesis: "zay-zay" and "a-zay, a-zay" are tuned rather to verbal whimsy than to fact)

. . . to the fact which, giving it reality, by its own reality establishes its own freedom from the necessity of the word, thus freeing it and dynamizing it at the same time.

This appears to mean that experience which has to be talked

into shape is suspect ("No ideas but in things," ran a later aphorism). Here, nearly two decades before Wallace Stevens spoke of the function of "noble imagery"—"A man without existing conventions (beliefs, etc.) depends for ideas of a new and noble order on 'noble imagery' "—Williams was flatly denying that poetry is meant to serve that function. The given world is *there*. It is neither a blank for our talk to fill, an amorphism for our words to shape, nor a disappointment for "noble imagery" to transfigure. This naïve realism, through which any philosopher would promptly drive a Mack truck, sufficed, for Williams, to free the poet from anxieties he hadn't the patience for. For him, the virtue of the given world, where rain for instance falls on red wheelbarrows, is that it can get on quite nicely without our expressive efforts:

A world detached from the necessity of recording it, sufficient to itself, removed from him [i.e. from the poet] . . . with which he has bitter and delicious relations and from which he is independent.

—such a world he does not carry "like a bag of food," nor invoke as the ground of familiarity between himself and readers; rather he values it "because it possesses the quality of independent existence, of reality which we feel in ourselves. It is not opposed to art but apposed to it."

Whence, finally,

Sometimes I speak of imagination as a force, an electricity or a medium, a place. It is immaterial which: for whether it is the condition of a place or a dynamization its effect is the same: to free the world of fact from the impositions of "art" . . . and to liberate the man to act in whatever direction his disposition leads.

And all this discussion has had no effect whatever, whereas certain phrases of Eliot's have been of immense effect. A practical reason is that Williams' book was published, 300 copies only, in paper covers, by a little expatriate house in Paris, whereas Eliot's *Sacred Wood* had the availability Methuen & Co.'s imprint could confer. A more pertinent reason is that Williams had no idea how to arrange and phrase what he wanted to say. Pound meant something like this when he called his old friend "*the* most bloody inarticulate animal that ever gargled." He was writing homemade philosophy, and floundered as grievously explaining the Imagination in the 1920's as he did explaining his other discovery, the Variable Foot, in the 1950's. Yet as on a stage where we see nothing a good mime leaning on the invisible mantelpiece can persuade us he knows where the fireplace would be, so Williams' gesturings around the Imagination are not random nor self-contradictory but compatible with the existence, located and perceived by him, of a reality he may not succeed in making us see.

What goaded Williams into much cerebration—and helped him for the first time to write poem after poem as if he knew what he was trying to do—was the presence and celebrity of *The Waste Land*. His response to *The Waste Land* was immediate and visceral: it was a going *back*, in his opinion; it was even (he did not avoid melodramatic terms) an act of betrayal. After a third of a century had passed, the mention of Eliot could still stir up in him a blind indignation. In 1956, having heard somewhere that "The Hippopotamus" bore some relation to Gautier's "L'Hippopotame," he was asserting to visitors that it was "a translation"—his voice rose to an indignant break on this word—and expressing blank amazement that a man would pass off another's poem as his own "without even an acknowledgment." So much had *The Waste Land* festered in his memory: the very emblem of radical evasiveness. Why?

The Waste Land was no doubt ideologically offensive, colliding as it did with his American optimism. But it was poetically offensive, and that was worse. It invaded and availed itself of the British literary tradition, an alien tradition, to exploit for itself that tradition's vast prestige. That was indeed the unforgivable sin. For, making all things new, American poets had the obligation to disentangle a native tradition, even if that meant setting word after word as though there had never been poetry before.

> —*in a hundred years, perhaps—*
> *the syllables*
> > *(with genius)*
> > > *or perhaps*
> *two lifetimes*
>
> *Sometimes it takes longer*

In the offense *The Waste Land* gave by its novelty, Williams saw (accurately enough) a novelty of the surface, giving scandal by jagged transitions between passages as Websterian or as Tennysonian as academia might please. He intuited the ease with which, once gotten used to, it would take its place (as it has) among older poems in anthologies that commence with Chaucer. But Williams wanted the new American poetry to open a new anthology entirely. It was his brooding about this New World Scripture that brought him to his late insistence on the American Idiom and the Variable Foot.

Wallace Stevens cared about poetry, not about *new* poetry; this is an important distinction. Unlike T. S. Eliot, however, he seems not to have much meditated the relation of himself to poetry, of the Individual Talent to Tradition. So with none of Williams' ferocity of technical perception (the struts and connectors fabricated as though by arc-light) he accepted poetic texture, poetic eloquence, more or less as it came to him from reading, content to characterize its mood in a lecture title, "The Noble Rider and the Sound of Words." His recorded musings, within his poems or alongside them, are not about how one may put poems together.

They are about Life. Without "the sexual myth," he wrote, without "the human revery or poem of death," we should be —hold on—"Castratos of moon-mash."

> *Life consists*
> *Of propositions about life. The human*
>
> *Revery is a solitude in which*
> *We compose these propositions, torn by dreams,*
>
> *By the terrible incantations of defeats*
> *And by the fear that defeats and dreams are one.*
>
> *The whole race is a poet that writes down*
> *The eccentric propositions of its fate.*

—Try *that* on the seminar. Ideas, ideas. The poetry, neatly but not arrestingly shaped, holds them, efficiently suspended, for discussion.

His eloquence, irresistible to the quoter, is aroused by its own self-sufficient replacement of what one at first supposes it is "about." Take his most famous evocation of his Muse:

> *It was her voice that made*
> *The sky acutest at its vanishing.*
> *She measured to the hour its solitude.*
> *She was the single artificer of the world*
> *In which she sang. And when she sang, the sea,*
> *Whatever self it had, became the self*
> *That was her song, for she was the maker. Then we,*
> *As we beheld her striding there alone,*
> *Knew that there never was a world for her*
> *Except the one she sang and, singing, made.*

Her song absorbs the neutral "given" world: sea, sky and hour grown gossamer-light, to be taken into song. They offered little noticeable resistance.

> *The ever-hooded, tragic-gestured sea*
> *Was merely a place by which she walked to sing,*

and

> *The meaningless plungings of water and the wind*

were phenomena among phenomena, such phenomena as voices, hers and ours. For her song exceeds her voice; her song is not "sound alone" but intention, ordered intention, intended order, order *exacted* by a meaninglessness that seemed meaningful once when Homer encountered it and maybe thought to borrow the sea's low sound for the line in which Odysseus walks despairing by the sea,

> . . . para thina poluphloisboio thalasses,

which Robert Fitzgerald renders

> *beside the endless wash of the wide, wide sea,*
> *weary and desolate as the sea.*

A Noble Rider, Homer, but also a noble sea, something godly for the mind to encounter as more than equal, and borrow eloquence from.

But the sea's sound seems godly no more, merely acoustic and hydraulic, and to talk about Homer's transactions with it now seems a Tennysonian fallacy. For Stevens the sea, the sky, the given world are accordingly loose, blank, to be dealt with arbitrarily. It is not upon any benison of what is not human that "so much depends." If this state of poetic affairs is a kind of bankruptcy, much literary history since 1700 may be read as a set of account books, detailing its stages. Even Augustan poets had occasional moments of vertigo, when the whole inherited corpus of poetry seemed a set of *effects*, like fireworks or neon signs, all potentially affecting, all potentially a little absurd. ("And China's earth receives the smoking tide"—tea going into a cup. Pope is teasing us, but with an alarming possibility, the possibility that noble imagery may enunciate nonsense.) Poetry can be radically absurd because radically irrelevant to what men had come to think the world they knew came down to: matter in motion, received through the blank eye. That left the poet to enhance it with supreme fictions, not always luckily. Johnson's friend James Grainger, who celebrated in verse the culture of the sugar-cane, commenced a new section, "Now Muse, let's sing of Rats," and Johnson himself disfigured a noble poem with the lines,

> *Forgive my transports on a theme like this;*
> *I cannot bear a French metropolis,*

and later still, in 1864, we find Tennyson writing of "ocean-spoil / In ocean-smelling osier," because the requirements of an enhancing rhythm will not accommodate the mention of fish in a basket. For more than two centuries the elevated verse of the Noble Rider has moved uncomfortably close to the ridiculous. The verse, and all its rhetorical convolutions, belong to an autonomous verse tradition. You learn to write it by reading what others have written. But learning to write it no longer teaches you to *see*, because its way of seeing ("Blow, winds, and crack your cheeks") is no longer believed in. That belief past, the things you write about, or "about," belong to the silent universe of no persons and no speech, somewhere "out there." Tennyson's friend Edward Lear at length perceived that the safest course for poetry, since its ligatures with phenomena were causing it so much trouble, was to shut itself up completely in its own cocoon of suggestion, celebrating the exploits not of rats and fish (not to mention winds and trees and men) but of the Dong with the Luminous Nose and the Land where the Jumblies Live, as it were lands where people with strange hats bear those unforgettable Stevens names, Mrs. Alfred Uruguay, Canon Aspirin, Professor Eucalyptus.

"One sits and beats an old tin can, lard pail," says Stevens' Man on the Dump; is it then "a philosopher's honeymoon," is it in fact the art of poetry,

> *to sit among mattresses of the dead,*
> *Bottles, pots, shoes and grass and murmur* aptest eve:
> *Is it to hear the blatter of grackles and say*
> Invisible priest; *is it to eject, to pull*
> *The day to pieces and cry* stanza my stone?

An early Stevens poem called "Anecdote of Canna" has just nine lines and has the following to say:

> *Huge are the canna in the dreams of*
> *X, the mighty thought, the mighty man.*
> *They fill the terrace of his capitol.*
>
> *His thought sleeps not. Yet thought that wakes*
> *In sleep may never meet another thought*
> *Or thing. . . . Now day-break comes . . .*
>
> *X promenades the dewy stones,*
> *Observes the canna with a clinging eye,*
> *Observes and then continues to observe.*

This is "about," as it were, Romanticism, where we have a sleeping world, dominated by thoughts and dreams, and a waking world, dominated by the eye. Both contain a man with no name; being rather a datum than a person, he is called X. In the sleeping world he is "the mighty thought, the mighty man." In the sleeping world the lavish flowers are "huge," and he has a capitol (being a mighty man; it is amusing to learn from a letter that Stevens had the President in mind—Wilson? Harding?), and the flowers fill his capitol's terrace, and his thought sleeps not. But just as the poem seems to be gathering itself for some extravagance of heroic statement, "daybreak comes." And in the daylit world? In the daylit world,

> *X promenades the dewy stones,*
> *Observes the canna with a clinging eye,*
> *Observes and then continues to observe.*

Observes and then continues to observe, as the poem quickly discovers that there is really nothing more for a poem to do. There was just a possibility of a poem, and a ranting mounting huffe-snuffe poem, in the universe before daybreak; but the observing eye killeth.

Every agnostic supposes he is the first, and Stevens talked as though his theme were the agnostic's plight. "The author's work," he wrote in 1954 on being asked for a summary statement, "suggests the possibility of a supreme fiction, recognized as a fiction, in which men could propose to themselves a fulfillment. In the creation of any such fiction, poetry would have a vital significance. There are many poems relating to the interactions between reality and the imagination, which are to be regarded as marginal to this central theme." Matthew Arnold was saying similar things in 1880:

> More and more mankind will discover that we have to turn to poetry to interpret life for us, to console us, to sustain us. Without poetry, our science will appear incomplete; and most of what now passes with us for religion and philosophy will be replaced by poetry.

Stevens took the dissolution of a Christianity inculcated in Reading, Pa., for the summons to a new humanism, a life's work. But his work illustrates more interestingly a phase in the history of poetry, to which he seems to have given little explicit attention, than in the history of philosophy and religion, concerning which he ruminated a great deal.

If for instance the Supreme Fiction has a supreme reality before which the ordinary given must make way—

> *In the way you speak*
> *You arrange, the thing is posed,*
> *What in nature merely grows*

—this the Symbolists before him had already postulated ("the dense wood of the trees," thought Mallarmé, must be dissolved into "the horror of the forest") and they in turn had learned it from Poe, who gives many hints on how Supreme Fictions may be constructed. You devise a Supreme Effect, Poe said, and proceed to a suitable meter, and finally hunt up words, and if your poem must contain a raven and a bust of Pallas, that will not be out of any obligation to existing ravens and marble, but in accord with your schemata of effects. Such Symbolists as learned English—Mallarmé did—solely for the purpose of reading the great Poe were deceived, we incline to think. They thought, so to speak, that they were reading Wallace Stevens. Stevens deserves that honor. His word-wizardry is what Poe's was thought to be: a kind of poetry, in the English language, which some very subtle and impassioned Frenchmen intuited.

Now when the given has made way for the poem, people who fancy themselves connoisseurs of the given—payers of its taxes, after all, hirers of its house-painters—are apt to protest, not always pertinently:

> They said, "*You have a blue guitar,*
> *You do not play things as they are.*"

And the poet is likely to take up the banter in their terms:

> The man replied, "*Things as they are*
> *Are changed upon the blue guitar.*" ·

Yet despite his smart riposte the people have a point. All that upon which they feel that "so much depends" is somehow emptied out, and if they complain about the color of the guitar their real dissatisfaction is with that emptying.

For how should a guitarist go about playing "things as they are"? Stevens has chosen aestheticism's ground with care. Upon any guitar, "things as they are" would be changed, by the transposition of thingness and thingly relationships into sounds and sonoric relationships; and what inflection of so radical a change might blue paint on the guitar impart? We should not expect to be able to formulate an answer, though any bright freshman could draft a commentary. Art, it might run, is radically *other*; in some mysterious sense of "imitation," it imitates a reality it cannot replicate and—people always need to be told—does not venture to replicate. (Why, for that matter, should one want a second reality just like the first?) The seminar's straight man is ready:

—For the sake of having it indoors. It is winter, but here by my fire I wish for green summer trees.

—Then they will be trees of the Imagination.

—Doubtless; but can you not arrange that they give me the satisfactions of non-imaginary trees?

—That cannot be arranged. "The difference between art and the event is always absolute."

—Who said so?

—T. S. Eliot said so; and by implication Aristotle before him.

—I am crushed.

For Aristotle in a passage little noticed did say that the dancer by rhythm alone, "by the rhythms of his attitudes," may represent men's characters, as well as what men do and suffer, and the distinction between the dancer and the doer is not to be easily traversed. The flute-player and the lyre-player too, he said, imitate these things, though with harmony as well as rhythm; and other imitators use color and form, and others use words. All these imitate.

But regardless of their means, what they imitate, Aristotle stresses, is Action: "actions, with agents who are necessarily either good or bad." He says nothing about the merely physical, merely visible world, which appears to be the connotation of Stevens' "things as they are." Furthermore—this gets more interesting—you will search Stevens' canon in vain for human actions with agents good and bad. You will find the likes of Cotton and Sly, barely there except to embody the vocative case, and the man who desires them to tell him of the eagle. That man, that speaker, is unusually assertive for a Stevens voice. You will find Crispin, of whom you can discover little, and the woman taking coffee of a Sunday morning, who dreams a little, and says two short things, and hears a voice say something enigmatic, but is otherwise as still as an Odalisque of Matisse is still upon the canvas. There is a great deal of language in these poems, with no one speaking it except the grave impersonal voice of poetry, and there is little variety of feeling. The most that happens is that the voice turns whimsical. That grave equable voice, as dispassionate as *things*, weaves its whimsical monologue; Crispin and Mrs. Pappadopoulos and Mrs. Alfred Uruguay and other improbable folk are nodes in the monologue. In fact, Mrs. Pappadopoulos seems to have been hired, like an art-school model, for the purposes of a demonstration in which she impersonates "This mechanism, this apparition," reclining on her elbow in a life-class pose while the lecturer prates of Projection A and Projection C. *She* does not signify.

So it is possible that Aristotle is not of much direct help. The Stevens world is empty of people. That is because he is in the Wordsworth line, a Nature Poet, confronting an emptied Nature, but a Nature without Presences, no longer speaking. For a poet closer to Stevens than Wordsworth is, William Cullen Bryant, nature had still been eloquent:

> *To him who in the love of Nature holds*
> *Communion with her visible forms, she speaks*
> *A various language; for his gayer hours*
> *She has a voice of gladness, and a smile*
> *And eloquence of beauty, and she glides*
> *Into his darker musings, with a mild*
> *And healing sympathy, that steals away*
> *Their sharpness, ere he is aware.*

When thoughts "of the last bitter hour" arise to trouble us, Nature's eloquence is still our resource:

> *Go forth, under the open sky, and list*
> *To Nature's teachings, while from all around—*
> *Earth and her waters, and the depths of air—*
> *Comes a still voice:—*

—and the rest of "Thanatopsis" is what that voice has to say. As it speaks, Bryant's verse plays a liturgical trick,

getting repeatedly a dying fall from end-stopped lines which
it interpolates into the lists it produces in enjambed lines:

> *The hills*
> *Rock-ribbed and ancient as the sun—the vales*
> *Stretching in pensive quietness between;*
> *The venerable woods—rivers that move*
> *In majesty, and the complaining brooks*
> *That make the meadows green; and, poured round all,*
> *Old Ocean's gray and melancholy waste,—*

a rhetoric of melancholy Stevens also exploits:

> *Although she strews the leaves*
> *Of sure obliteration on our paths,*
> *The path sick sorrow took, the many paths*
> *Where triumph rang its brassy phrase, or love*
> *Whispered a little out of tenderness . . .*

This is from "Sunday Morning," of course, that consigning
of Christianity to the dead, which refers each of the woman's
queries to Nature and does not let Nature speak, Nature
being too self-sufficient, but instead very tactfully speaks in
Nature's behalf. "Divinity," the poem's voice tells the
woman, "must live within herself:"

> *Passions of rain, or moods in falling snow;*
> *Grievings in loneliness, or unsubdued*
> *Elations when the forest blooms; gusty*
> *Emotions on wet roads on autumn nights;*
> *All pleasures and all pains, remembering*
> *The bough of summer and the winter branch.*
> *These are the measures destined for her soul.*

They are all her responsibility, these emotions, though
catalyzed by liquids, gases, cellulose structures; not emotions Nature will enact for her instruction. Bryant's is a
spasmodic eloquence, Stevens' a suavely mannered. They
improvise at the same pace, on related themes, in the same
key. Only the locus of the passion shifts.

The great novelty of "Sunday Morning," however, is

not its modification of Bryant's sentiments; the great novelty is the way the poem opens not into a world, still tenuously Aristotle's, of place and person, but into a becalmed world of visual arrangement: Painting.

> *Complacencies of the peignoir, and late*
> *Coffee and oranges in a sunny chair,*
> *And the green freedom of a cockatoo*
> *Upon a rug mingle to dissipate*
> *The holy hush of ancient sacrifice.*

A Matisse designing with orange upon green, content with sunlight, rugs, breakfast things, a cocktatoo, is implicitly contrasted with the Old Master—unnecessary to specify one—whom a long tradition of sacred subjects coerces. The post-Impressionist flaunts a scandalous freedom. Pictures now (1916) caress the seen world. And Stevens introduces his woman as though she were part of such a painting, herself a sensuousness, scandalously free; and he distances her reverie to the plane where we may imagine people in highly stylized paintings having thoughts. If you imagine a painted woman having thoughts, you are passing (it is hard to say how far) beyond any intent of the painter. The eye is caressed by appearance, arranged appearance, appearance arranged within art's silent world. "The Man with the Blue Guitar" in the same way takes off from the Picasso of the blue landscapes and emaciated harlequins, and offers the unplayed music, silent speech, unstatable statement which, obligated by the pressure of Picasso's vision, might be expected to issue from a guitar in a painted universe.

This may be Stevens' chief technical insight. Very early in his career he appears to have sensed that in the time since Wordsworth's enterprise foundered it has been the painter who has developed the only feasible relationship of the sole man to the mute universe. The painter's works cling to its dimension, the visual, and share its muteness. Pictures do with the visible universe what poetry once did with the universe the visible universe superseded, the universe of speech, which traced everything to the *logos* and heard everything informed with divine and human voices (for Bryant the voice of Nature is a convention, vestigial). So Stevens allows the painter to precede him, performing the first selection, the first arrangement, the first concretion of images. The strange dimension in which his language operates, employing in recognizable sentence patterns words you can look up if you don't happen to recognize them, always seeming to be saying in an orderly way something really simple which we find we cannot quite follow, is accounted for and perhaps obliged by the metaphor of the painting: familiar language transmuted into a self-contained system by exactly the same means Picasso has employed in transmuting familiar visual facts into a self-contained system: language caught up into the world of the painted guitar.

Which is why, in Stevens' world, there are no actions and no speeches, merely ways of looking at things. The long tradition of mimesis uses words to imitate actions and speeches; but confronted by a world of matter and motion, from which actions and speeches have departed, mimesis can only imitate (1) old poems, or (2) the movements of the mind transposing and reconstituting what is seen. Old poems Stevens frequently imitates, their way, their air, their rituals. The movements of the transposing, reconstituting mind, these he imitates habitually, and it is frequently the movements of the painter's mind that he elects as model. And so we have a poem called "Thirteen Ways of Looking at a Blackbird."

Stevens might have invented the Blackbird. It performs no Aristotelian actions: in ways accessible to poetry, it neither does nor suffers. You could not write a tragedy about it. It is presumably sentient, yet alien; yet not more alien, in the cosmos of Newton, than any other sentient thing: than Mrs. Pappadopoulos, say, or the Friends from Pascagoula. And the blackbird is alien from the kingdom of traditional poetry, where he obtains a visa only as part of the company baked in a pie; and alien also from that sphere of feeling which Wordsworth denominated "Nature." No sense sublime of something far more deeply interfused has its dwelling, so far as we intuit, in him. He will serve very nicely as the projection into art's cosmos of the Solitary (archetype of Wordsworth's Leech Gatherer): instantly visible, the inevitable focus of attention in any picture or poem in which he appears, a black shape, a hoarse cry. Hence Variation I:

> *Among twenty snowy mountains*
> *The only moving thing*
> *Was the eye of the blackbird.*

Merely detaching the blackbird from the background, this is the first way of looking; the remaining twelve devise context after context for this ineradicable black flaw on the mind's purity.

> *I was of three minds,*

says the second one,

> *Like a tree*
> *In which there are three blackbirds.*

This is to compare the nagging presence of blackbirds, three of them, to a nagging dividedness of intention or attention. The eighth says,

> *I know noble accents*
> *And lucid, inescapable rhythms;*
> *But I know, too,*
> *That the blackbird is involved*
> *In what I know.*

"Out, damn'd spot," thinks the will; but he will not out; in the ninth variation,

> *When the blackbird flew out of sight,*
> *It marked the edge*
> *Of one of many circles.*

—filling the sky, filling the mind, with a whole Copernican apparatus. For this is a comic poem, essentially comic in the austerity with which it allows the blackbird to nag at it. Thinking to evade the persistent bird, we may improvise an utterly fantastic world; we may begin, for example,

> *He rode over Connecticut*
> *In a glass coach.*

Alas, the dirty bird: our bubble is no sooner blown than the indomitable blackbird turns up inside it:

> *He rode over Connecticut*
> *In a glass coach.*
> *Once, a fear pierced him,*
> *In that he mistook*
> *The shadow of his equipage*
> *For blackbirds.*

The thirteenth way, its turns out, is simply to look:

> *It was evening all afternoon.*
> *It was snowing*
> *And it was going to snow.*
> *The blackbird sat*
> *In the cedar-limbs.*

At any rate it looks like a simple looking. It is quite as peculiar as any of the preceding twelve; there are three declarative sentences, each one turning on a slight logical puzzle, and the third is about a blackbird, and we are meant to find some way of relating them. If we are not conscious of any difficulty in doing this, that is because of our experience with the coincidences of the visible universe, where dark snowy afternoons and blackbirds often engage in mutual coexistence. This sequence of words no more holds up the mirror to Nature than did any of the preceding ones. But for once a correspondence of two *Gestalts*, this of words, that of natural things, can persuade us that dissonances have been dissolved. Language, it would seem, can mime the wordless world only by a kind of coincidence, as when a stain on the wallpaper resembles a face. The sequence coheres by postulating a maximal separation between what is said and what is experienced, so that it can produce a climactic flat recognition by making their contours momentarily coincide. This assumption is the polar opposite of Williams' assumption that words share thinghood with things, and that language is a social fact needing no explanations. A Williams poem becomes as unintelligible, if we make a puzzle of how words relate to reality, as a Stevens poem does if we do not.

Each of the thirteen ways of looking at a blackbird is a way of playing with the *word* blackbird, setting it in a miniature context, bounded by the shape of a stanza or the rules of a sentence, exactly as a painter might play with the *shape* blackbird, placing it somewhere within his rectangle among a gamut of accessories: trees, houses, glass coaches. Similarly when Williams made one of his "machines made out of words," the word "wheelbarrow," lifted off the plane on which things are being *said*, was one of the machine's components. But Williams does not expect us to reflect of his sharply visual wheelbarrow what Stevens cannot forget about his equally visual blackbirds. It is the norm of the Stevens poetic that if one of the pictures should resemble a blackbird sitting in cedar-limbs beneath snow on a lowering day, that picture is no less an arbitrary deed, no less a formal composition, than the most fanciful of the arrangements that precede it.

So many scrupulously arrested gestures, so laborious an honesty, such a pother of fine shades and nuanced distinctions; yet that forty years' work revolves about nothing more profound than bafflement with a speechless externality which poets can no longer pretend is animate. This fact invalidates no Stevens poem, only the terms on which some of the poems ask us to take them. In one bleak sense all

poems are nonsense poems (all statements nonsense statements?) since we can always refuse to be beguiled, can always point to an interweaving of vowels, a symmetry of
phrasing, a jingle of like endings, nothing *said*. No one understood this fact better than Stevens, who surpassed even
Eliot (rhymer of "grow old" and "trousers rolled") in his
plumbing of the resources of near-nonsense:

> *Pure coruscations, that lie beyond*
> *The imagination, intact*
> *And unattained . . .*
>
> *We enjoy the ithy oonts and long-haired*
> *Plomets, as the Herr Gott*
> *Enjoys his comets.*

"The word must be the thing it represents," he wrote;
"otherwise it is a symbol." Break loose, then, from repre-
sentation, and let the words be what they will, like the
words of Edward Lear, who has no symbols.

> *. . . By day*
> *The wood-dove used to chant his hoobla-hoo*
>
> *And still the grossest iridescence of ocean*
> *Howls hoo and rises and howls hoo and falls.*
> *Life's nonsense pierces us with strange relation.*

In those *Notes Toward a Supreme Fiction*, Stevens once
more is quite explicit about "The meaningless plungings of
water and the wind." They come down to "hoo": life's
nonsense. Words, it may be, come down to nothing much
better; a Frenchman's dog comes down to "chien." When
you think about foreign languages, as Stevens often did,
you understand how arbitrary is language.

He tended to suppose that he was at grips with a re-
ligious or a philosophic crisis. But it was a writers' crisis
purely, a poets' crisis, an episode in the history of nature
poetry since Wordsworth. It is entangled in religion and
philosophy: of course it is. But it existed, neatly, on the
poetic plane: how to make predications concerning snow,

or blackbirds. It was on the poetic plane that Stevens coped with it, often magnificently.

How a phase in the evolution of nature poetry since Wordsworth came to be epitomized by a Harvard man living in Hartford, Conn., is a question worth pondering. Why are Stevens' poems not populated, except by cartoon-like wisps?

One might sketch notes toward an answer by observing how few people, how little speech, the products of the American imagination have typically contained. People in a very large country, nomadic people, people who spend much time operating machinery ("lending it to no one," wrote Faulkner, "letting no other hand ever know the last secret forever chaste forever wanton intimacy of its pedals and levers"), people whose communication is shared work, not shared speech, in fact so self-conscious about their speech they needed persuading (by Mencken, in the 1920's) that they *had* a spoken idiom; people inheriting the possibility that one might spend six months in one's cabin without sighting anyone fit to be spoken to; people who find nothing strange in the life style of Thoreau, who throve on the self-containment that drove Robinson Crusoe nearly mad; people whose sages almost within living memory shuttled from lecture platform to lecture platform, and who spend more of their lives listening to schoolteachers than any other people in the world, and who are addressed all their lives as *audiences* by the politician, the columnist, the barber; people who did not grow up anywhere near the neighbors they have at present, and approach them (when necessary, about a dog or a lawnmower) with embarrassed colloquial ceremony: such people find it easier on the whole to shape their emotions to the abstract or the inanimate. The legend of American violence means that trespassers on the psychic *Lebensraum* are most effectively addressed as settlers once addressed Indians, with a projectile. The legend of the inarticulate American hero—Nick Adams or Li'l

Abner—means that the precedents for addressing someone are scanty, and that is the meaning likewise of James' Mandarin style. (James addressed *himself*, as habitually as did Thoreau, and projected his ruminations into dialogue; only an American novelist could have arrived at such conventions for speech: "Oh, she didn't at all 'dart,' " I replied, "just now at me. I darted, much rather, at *her*.").

Pin down an American and he utters a quotation, said Ezra Pound after living for some time abroad; and the characters of that master of the urban colloquial, Scott Fitzgerald, make even their small talk out of quotations from magazines: just such magazines as printed Fitzgerald's stories. Speech for the writer—ignoring for the moment Faulkner, of the un-nomadic South—speech for the writer is something gleaned by fieldwork, something external; in that way Mark Twain, an incomparable monologist, discriminated five dialects in *Huckleberry Finn*, the indices of five classes. Communication is a "subject," formally studied; universities have Departments of Communication Skills. In no other country would it have been plausible for the telephone to be invented, which allows one to enter another's house without the ceremonies of entrance or introduction, and moreover without actually going there; and Claude Shannon in the telephone company's laboratories has constructed of Communication a mathematical model which measures Improbability invading Randomness, assisted by Redundancy to offset mistakes: could any European have thought of that? James and Stevens help you intuit it: configurations, unlikely configurations, gathering slowly out of what seems a random cloud. And in Stevens' longest poem the letter C, including "all related or derivative sounds, for instance *X*, *TS* and *Z*," encode an unperson named Crispin, like, Stevens said, "the sounds of the crickets, etc." accompanying St. Francis. "Sometimes the sounds squeak all over the place, as, for example, in the line 'Exchequering from piebald fiscs unkeyed.' The word exchequering is about as full of the sounds of C as any word that I can think of." The crickets were not St. Francis, but that cloud of palatal and alveolar redundancies in a very real sense *is* Crispin, ghost in a clattering machine.

William Carlos Williams approached the domain of speech differently. Practicing medicine, he spent much of each day of his life with people who had a desperate need to tell him something. His ear for compelled speech was nearly absolute:

> *Will you please rush down and see*
> *ma baby. You know, the one I talked*
> *to you about last night*
>
> *What was that?*
>
> *Is this the baby specialist?*
>
> *Yes, but perhaps you mean my son,*
> *can't you wait until   .   ?*
>
> *I, I, I don't think it's brEAthin'*

A fieldwork note; and when he writes prose dialogue it rings as if transcribed; Williams was not, like Dickens or like Faulkner, an *impersonator*. But the habit of listening to voices extended to his own voice, so that he could write down the way he heard himself phrasing things:

THE POEM

> *It's all in*
> *the sound. A song.*
> *Seldom a song. It should*
>
> *be a song—made of*
> *particulars, wasps,*
> *a gentian—something*
> *immediate, open*

> scissors, *a lady's*
> *eyes—waking*
> *centrifugal, centripetal*

You hear the staccato phrasing of a taut voice. You also hear things speech wouldn't know how to clarify: the auditory relationships in

> *sound. A song.*
> *Seldom a song. It should*
>
> *be a song—*

with the white space prolonging the tension after "should"; and "open" floating between "immediate," which it clarifies, and "scissors," which it specifies (the delay of the white space again withholding "scissors" till we've had time to take "open" with "immediate"). "A lady's," similarly, seems to go with "scissors" till round the corner of the line we encounter "eyes," and the last two words—"centrifugal, centripetal"—seem to tell us how the lady's wakened attention turns outward then inward, until we remember the title and think to include "centrifugal, centripetal" among the specifications for "The Poem." It's not "oral," it's too quirky and tricky for orality, but one of its qualifications for anatomizing its theme is that it knows what a voice sounds like.

It's not only not "oral," this poem, it's not fully present, not even quite intelligible, in being read aloud, nor yet in being looked at on the page. It's an audio-visual counterpoint, and "the Imagination" Williams talked about is as good a name as any for the region where the complete poem can be said to exist.

This ability to move close to quite simple words, both hearing them spoken—not quite the same thing as hearing their sounds—and seeing them interact on a typewritten page, gave Williams the sense of constant discovery that saved him from feeling constantly responsible for weighty problems. He liked a poem he could spin round on one corner, and it freed him not to be encumbered with pronouncements. He typed and retyped sequences of a few dozen words, changing a word or two, or shifting the point in a phrase at which the eye must turn back round a line's end. "No ideas but in things" meant that the energy moving from word to word would be like that of the eye moving from thing to thing, and not like that of the predicating faculty with its opinions:

> —*through metaphor to reconcile*
> *the people and the stones.*
> *Compose. (No ideas*
> *but in things) Invent!*
> *Saxifrage is my flower that splits*
> *the rocks.*

The same poem tells us that the writing is to be of words; he never supposed that "things" got onto the page. And "Saxifrage is my flower": though he did not need the convention that Nature was speaking, he was untroubled by any sense of its remote exteriority because he sensed his own biological kinship with processes of struggle and growth. A way to be part of the world is to consider that through the world as through yourself moves the energy of a cellular dance: not much of an "idea" as ideas go, but true enough to get many poems out of.

> *. . . The petals!*
> *the petals undone*
> *loosen all five and*
> *swing up*
>
> *The flower*
> *flows to release—*
>
> *Fast within a ring*
> *where the compact*
> *agencies*
> *of conception*
>
> *lie mathematically*
> *ranged*

round the
hair-like sting—

From such a pit
the color flows
over
a purple rim

upward to
the light! the light!
all around— . . .

Helped out by experiences Wordsworth couldn't have—
time-lapse films of opening flowers, and a biology of dynamics, not of classifications—this kind of writing about
natural process belongs to a new phase in the history of
poetry. To a reader of professional books on nutrition and
mitosis, "Nature" meant something both intimate and
thrusting.

Process: growth and emergence: these were his themes:
the effort of the new organism to define itself. They were
comprised in what he meant by spring, by flowers and buds,
by the "American idiom" (something *new*), by the effort
at communal self-definition he discovered and re-enacted *In
the American Grain*. Birth, for the obstetrician-poet, was
the triumphant moment, not an instant beginning but the
culmination of something nine months or nine millennia pre-
pared. "She entered, as Venus from the sea, dripping": so he
began a novel. "The air enclosed her, she felt it all over her,
touching, waking her. If Venus did not cry aloud after release from the pressures of that sea-womb, feeling the new
and lighter flood springing in her chest, flinging out her
arms—this one did. Screwing up her tiny smeared face, she
let out three convulsive yells—and lay still."

The struggle to get born, that was always Williams'
plot; flowers fascinated him because they achieved it visibly,
effortlessly. And then—the other half of his plot—the closure
of the prison-house, as in Wordsworth and Blake, round the
newborn potentiality. That prison-house—he is closer to

Blake than to Wordsworth—is a communal failure, the lapsed Imagination. How do men think so little of themselves that they put up with what they put up with?

> *She stirs, distraught,*
> *against him—wounded (drunk), moves*
> *against him (a lump) desiring,*
> *against him, bored   .*
>
> *flagrantly bored and sleeping, a*
> *beer-bottle still grasped spear-like*
> *in his hand   .*
>
> *while the small, sleepless boys, who*
> *have climbed the columnar rocks*
> *overhanging the pair (where they lie*
> *overt upon the grass, besieged—*
>
> *careless in their narrow cell under*
> *the crowd's feet) stare down,*
> *   from history!*
> *at them, puzzled and in the sexless*
> *light (of childhood) bored equally,*
> *go charging off   .*

All these people once entered "as Venus from the sea, dripping," the boys more recently, and as for the boys, if they now look down "from history," they perhaps will be looked down upon in turn when their present sexlessness has become desire. Is that all anybody can imagine? Citizen of a country that can remember its beginnings, he looked (like his classmate Pound) for a point of failure in history: no metaphysical wound (for the flowers with which we share life are not wounded) but a failure of vision, a lapsing of the Imagination. Hence his interest in the past of Paterson (which was never anything but a company town), and his singling out of the moment when "they saw birds with rusty breasts and called them robins."

Thus, from the start, an America of which they could have had no inkling drove the first settlers upon their past. . . . For what they saw were not robins. They were thrushes only vaguely resembling the rosy, daintier English bird. . . .

The example is slight but enough properly to incline the understanding. Strange and difficult, the new continent induced a torsion in the spirits of the first settlers, tearing them between the old and the new. And at once a split occurred in that impetus which should have carried them forward as one into the dangerous realities of the future. . . .

That is his myth of history, a birth rejected out of fear. His long career means that a poet needs no more ideas than that. (It is not made of ideas, said Mallarmé of poetry; it is made of words.) Chiefly a poet needs a passionate interest in the language, in the words people use, and the words they might use but do not. (And why do they not? Why is "torsion" not a word we hear spoken? It would fill one air-pocket.) What people say, what they do not say but might: that, related to a myth of history, was Williams' field of preoccupation. And the myth—remembering settlers who did not guess how much depended on what they should call the bird they chose to call "robin"—is written invisibly down the margins of his least pretentious poems, which affirm, again and again, no more than "how much depends": depends upon the act of finding a few dozen words, and upon their array once a poet has found them.

> . . . Look at
> what passes for the new.
> You will not find it there but in
> despised poems.
> It is difficult
> to get the news from poems
> yet men die miserably every day
> for lack
> of what is found there.

IV ⁄ Disliking It

Marianne Moore told *viva voce*, and surely more than once, the story of her visit to the zoo. A man from *Life* was there, by arrangement, to photograph her in acts of guarded friendship with such beasts as might offset, by their bizarre aloofness, her innocent self-sufficient face and cartwheel hat. What she chiefly remembered about the day was a man expounding the snakes to a party of children. She overheard what he said, and noted what he neglected to say: a libel by omission, which it seemed her duty to correct. So, "You must be sure to tell those children," she said, "that snakes are not cold and not slimy; that they are dry and just as warm as their surroundings. One need not hesitate to touch them." The man from *Life* saw his cue; he caused a large snake to be passed into the hands of Miss Moore.

And she did not flinch from her principle, though she had never handled a snake before. She accepted it. She was immediately asked what it felt like. And, faithful to a life-long discipline, she consulted her fingers, and the memories to which her fingers gave access, and pronounced simply, "Like rose petals." It was perhaps too poetic a remark to make its point, but she never allowed a fear of being thought poetic to deter her from accuracy. For she meant a resemblance of snakes to rose petals neither as a fancy nor as a simile, but as a virtual identity of tactile sensation: a species of wit gone into the fingertips: a tactile pun.

In her poems, things utter puns to the senses. These, registered in words, make odd corrugations on the linguistic surface. Thus her words note a certain sleepy cat's "prune-shaped head and alligator eyes," and identify in his whiskers "the shadbones regularly set about the mouth, to droop or rise / in unison like the porcupine's quills," and register him, awake, "Springing about with froglike accuracy": the frog and the cat being two creatures that land where they meant to.

This policy of accurate comparison, bringing, if need be, the prune, the alligator, the shad, the porcupine, the frog to the service of a discussion of a cat, does not worry about congruousness much as Braque did not worry about perspective, being intent on a different way of filling its elected spaces. Congruity, like perspective, deals in proportions within an overall view. Miss Moore's poems deal in many separate acts of attention, all close-up; optical puns, seen by snapshot, in a poetic normally governed by the eye, sometimes by the ears and fingers, ultimately by the moral sense. It is the poetic of the solitary observer, for whose situation the meaning of a word like "moral" needs redefining: her special move in the situation where we have already observed Stevens and Williams, confronted by a world that does not speak and seems to want *describing*. Man confronted by brute nature: that is her situation, and theirs, and Hemingway's and Frost's. Its etiology needs some looking into.

— — —

Dr. Johnson was impatient with "noble wild prospects," which exacted, so he thought, nothing of the mind. Boswell, somewhat younger, felt that he wanted to describe them: ruins, rocks, grandeurs. In a note to himself in his journal he confessed, however, to being very weak at it. This note points less to his private inadequacies than to the fact that there existed no descriptive tradition from which he might have learned. For the art of describing accurately the thing seen was developed, so far as it has been developed, almost wholly in the nineteenth century. Words can set things seen before the mind only by a system of analogies, and until quite recently no one had thought to want analogies for the experience of the eye as it passes along the contours or across the surfaces of the seen world.

Literature has long abounded in visual imagery, but that is not the same thing as description. When Shakespeare has Romeo say,

> *Night's candles are burnt out, and jocund day*
> *Stands tiptoe on the misty mountaintops,*

the visual imagery that is set before our minds does not offer to transcribe the experience of the eye. If you commission an artist to draw what Shakespeare is setting before the mind, you get Blake's painting *Glad Day*, which looks like a jocund youth but not like the sun rising. In the same way, "night's candles" suggests the elation of the mind, but not the eye's experience with a field of stars. From the time of Homer till the time of John Donne, Nature had been apprehended according to the forms of personal analogies, as a field of wills and forces. Written down as analytically as possible, this sense of things generated the physics by which each thing seeks its place and Nature abhors a vacuum, and written down as generously as possible, the world of moonlight sleeping on banks, winds cracking their cheeks, and the stars keeping their courses.

In so deeply humanized a world, the mere testimony of

the eye—organ of the sense that uniquely testifies to our separateness from things—had negligible power to declare the *otherness* of the visible; and even after the world had ceased to be felt in that way, some time in the seventeenth century, after the New Philosophy had put all in doubt, the eye did not instantly enforce such separations. Rather, poetic diction continued to trace the old paths, informing us that restless Sol had shot his ardent ray, and justifying itself by claims about sublimity and about fancy. Already by the 1720's Pope had sensed that the old language, in enlightened times, could only make fun of itself in a complicated fashion—

> *Mean while, declining from the Noon of Day,*
> *The Sun obliquely shoots his burning Ray;*
> *The hungry Judges soon the Sentence sign,*
> *And Wretches hang that Jury-men may Dine;*
> *The Merchant from th' Exchange returns in Peace,*
> *And the long Labours of the Toilet cease.*

For the real world of hungry judges, oblivious merchants, anxious debutantes, the real world, as distinguished from the one where poets see a sun with Apollo's bow, has been defined (created) by the new astronomy, which supplies a sun as indifferent as these citizens. Pope the satirist implies as much. Elsewhere, Pope at his most sententious remains a tireless personifier—

> *Another Age shall see the golden Ear*
> *Embrown the Slope, and nod on the Parterre. . . .*

It was not until the 1790's that the universe of Newton, about which there is much to record but really little to say, was admitted to serious poetry.

Wordsworth, of course, admitted it—Wordsworth, whose very model was Newton, the unspeaking sage: not generating utterances (except perhaps afterward, in tranquillity) but rather "voyaging through strange seas of thought, alone." And Wordsworth, seeking to come to terms with a world where no restless Sol puts forth an ardent

ray, but people are "Roll'd round in earth's diurnal course /
With rocks, and stones, and trees," sensed that in the
presence of such a universe one's traditional language could
register no more than one's feelings about it. And Wordsworth's is the traditional language. His diction retains the
trick of personifying, but a trick now excused by "as if":

> *This City now doth, like a garment, wear*
> *The beauty of the morning.*

(Shakespeare would not have inserted "like a garment").
And what is not personified will be merely listed:

> *silent, bare,*
> *Ships, towers, domes, theatres, and temples lie*
> *Open unto the fields, and to the sky;*
> *All bright and glittering in the smokeless air.*

The Westminster Bridge sonnet is partly about the bare
city and partly about the observer's emotions:

> *Ne'er saw I, never felt, a calm so deep!*

For this universe, as he was to reflect repeatedly, is one
whose meaning you half perceive and half create. Moreover,
it half creates you; and Wordsworth's principal subject
became "The Growth of a Poet's Soul." There, for some
decades, poetry let the matter rest.

No work of the imagination is ever abandoned. The task
of mediating with a universe now merely visible, now
merely *there*, was carried on: not by poets, who took to
orchestrating passion, but by painters and scientists. By
John Constable, then, whose theme is a drama perceptible
in the experience of the eye, experience imitated by the
brush; and (with less drama but much narrative about fieldwork) by geologists, who developed the art of natural description with the prime purpose of educating the reader's
eye so he could learn to see things for himself. Some of the
nineteenth century's finest energies flowed into demonstra-
tive pedagogy; people were to read in a new way, intimate,
surprising, the Book of Nature, a book of marvels. By the

time Sherlock Holmes was damning "the great unobservant
public, that could hardly tell a weaver by his tooth, or a
compositor by his left thumb," the tradition had seeped into
the *Strand* magazine. It was a Scottish geologist, Hugh
Miller, who composed the phrase Stephen Dedalus was to
draw from his treasure-house, "A day of dappled seaborn
clouds."* It was a Swiss naturalist, Louis Agassiz, who
carried verbal mimesis of the experience of the eye to such
a pitch that Ezra Pound (in whose visual world "light
shaves grass into emerald") was to set him in the sphere of
the fixed stars, and remark that he could teach "even a
literatus" to write. And a principal amateur geologist of the
nineteenth century, who spent thousands of pounds to collect rocks and gems, and gave his attention by turns to the
eye's experience amid natural things and its experience
amid the painted forms of a Constable or a Turner, was of
course John Ruskin.

The greatest thing a human soul ever does in this world is
to see something, and tell what it saw in a plain way. Hundreds
of people can talk for one who can think, but thousands can
think for one who can see. To see clearly is poetry, prophecy
and religion all in one.

Here we are at the threshold of Marianne Moore, who does
not raise her voice nor blur her language. We are being told
that Nature does not teach us by dramatic example, as the
Renaissance supposed, nor by stealing into our hearts in a
wise passiveness, as Wordsworth supposed, but by guiding
an act of perception and enunciation entered into with the
whole being: which act is a moral act, and exfoliates almost
casually into moral reflections. Now attend to Ruskin as
he describes a fir tree:

The Power of the tree . . . is in the dark, flat, solid tables
of leafage, which it holds out on its strong arms, curved slightly

* *The Testimony of the Rocks*, 1857, Lecture VI, though Miller
wrote "breeze-borne."

over them like shields, and spreading towards the extremity like a hand. It is vain to endeavour to paint the sharp, grassy, intricate leafage until this ruling form has been secured; and in the boughs that approach the spectator the foreshortening of it is just like that of a wide hill-country, ridge just rising over ridge in successive distances.

This is meant to help educate the eyes of painters, who without Ruskin to instruct them in seeing are apt to paint fir trees constructed like chandeliers. He is tracing the tree's visible gestures. The strong arms his fir tree holds out betoken no act of personification, in the manner of the tiptoe posture of Romeo's dawn. They are analogies for the eye retracing the gesture made in three-dimensional space by the piny branches. These arms hold out "dark, flat, solid tables of leafage," and these tables curve over the branches "like shields," and spread out toward the extremity "like a hand." They are foreshortened, furthermore, as they approach the spectator, like the ridges of "a wide hill-country." Arms, tables, shields, hands, hills are so many analogies for the experience of the eye, by which the painter's eye is to be educated, and the art critic's also. They do not constitute a recipe for a painter, who if he were to paint what Ruskin names would arrive at surrealism. He is to learn from what Ruskin names, and paint the tree, having learned at last how to see it; and this putting down of what he has learned to see will not be copying but "poetry, prophecy and religion all in one."

This tree of arms, shields, tables, hands and hills, like Marianne Moore's cat of porcupine, alligator, shad and prune and frog, is a tree of language, not of nature or of painting: it exists only on Ruskin's printed page. It got there by an effort of attention, commanding the resources of the whole being, that devised and traversed a half-dozen analogies, analogies not for a stolid tree but for a tree's fancied kinetic act, and the eye's act responding. And Marianne Moore's focal discovery was the poetic cat that exists only on the page. Ruskin did not discover this, being content to impersonate Isaiah.

Like prophecy since Isaiah, poetry since Homer has imitated a voice crying, and the literary imitation of the visual was involved, when that problem finally arose, in endless compromises because the visual is voiceless. But the printed page itself is as uncompromisingly mute as cats and trees. It became the poet's medium when poets began to use typewriters.

At various times in her lifetime we discern Miss Moore being a librarian, an editor, a teacher of typewriting: locating fragments already printed; picking and choosing; making, letter by letter, neat pages. So one might itemize her poetic procedure.

Her poems are not for the voice; she sensed this in reading them badly. In response to a question, she once said that she wrote them for people to look at. Moreover, one cannot imagine them handwritten. As Ruskin's tree, on the page, exists in tension between arboreal process and the mind's serial inventory of arms, shields, tables, hands and hills, so Miss Moore's cats, her fish, her pangolins and ostriches exist on the page in tension between the mechanisms of print and the presence of a person behind those mechanisms. Handwriting flows with the voice, and here the voice is as synthetic as the cat, not something an elocutionist can modulate. The words on these pages are little regular blocks, set apart by spaces, and referrable less to the voice than to the click of the keys and the ratcheting of the carriage.

The stanzas lie on the page, one below another, in little intricate grids of visual symmetry, the left margin indented according to complex rules which govern the setting of tabulator stops. The lines obey no rhythmic system the ear can apprehend. We learn that there is a system not by listening but by counting syllables, and we find that the words are fixed within a grid of numerical rules. Thus "The Fish" has twenty-seven syllables per stanza, arranged in five lines on a three-part scheme of indentation, the syllables apportioned among the lines 1, 3, 9, 6, 8. (In the last line of stanza one, "opening" has two syllables.) And since a mosaic has no point of beginning, the poem is generated from somewhere just outside its own rigidly plotted field: generated less by ichthyological reality than by two words: "The Fish," which are part of the first sentence but not part of the symmetrical pattern, being in fact the poem's title. Therefore:

THE FISH

> *wade*
> *through black jade.*
>> *Of the crow-blue mussel-shells, one keeps*
>> *adjusting the ash-heaps;*
>>> *opening and shutting itself like*
> *an*
> *injured fan.*

To begin this sentence we read the title, and to end it we read three words (four syllables) of the next stanza: for the single stanza is a patterned zone specified within, but not coterminous with, the articulation of the sentences. The single stanza exhibits an archaic disregard of the mere things human desire does with sentences. The voice shaping sentences is anxious to be understood; these stanzas are cut and laminated in severe corrective to that anxiety, posing against it their authority of number (1, 3, 9, 6, 8) and typography. They even evade the sounds of speech with their rhymes, not performing, however, the traditional offices of rhymes, not miming a symmetry, clinching an epigram or caressing a melodic fluid, but cutting, cutting, cutting, with implacable arbitrariness: "like / an / injured fan."

It is a poem to see with the eye, conceived in a typewriter upon an 8½″ x 11″ sheet of paper. If metric is a system of emphases, centered in human comfort, human hope, syllable count is a system of zoning, implied by the *objectivity* of the words, which lie side by side for their syllables to be counted. If the stanzas of "Go, lovely rose" are primarily audible, created by the symmetries of the uttering voice, the stanzas of "The Fish" are primarily visible, created by an arrangement of words in typographic space, the poem made for us to look at. Miss Moore could even revise a poem from beginning to end without changing a word in it. The first three times "The Fish" appeared in print its stanzaic system grouped the syllables not 1, 3, 9, 6, 8 but 1, 3, 8, 1, 6, 8, and in six lines, not five:

THE FISH

wade
through black jade.
　Of the crow-blue mussel-shells, one
　　keeps
　　adjusting the ash heaps;
　opening and shutting itself like
an
injured fan.

What readers have been looking at since 1930 is a revised version. The poem was twelve years old when the author made this change, and, despite the mechanical ease of retyping, it is not a trivial change, since it affects the system by which pattern intersects utterance, alters the points at which the intersections occur, provides a new grid of impediments to the over-anxious voice, and modifies, moreover, the intrusiveness of the system itself: the new version actually relents a little its self-sufficient arbitrariness, and consigns more leisurely fish to only half as many winking little quick monosyllabic turns. We can nearly say that we have a *new* poem, arrived at in public and without changing a word, by applying a system of transformations to an existing poem. We may remember Charles Ives's statement that American music is *already written* (he had no need to invent tunes), and his "What has music to do with *sound*?", as who should ask, what has poetry to do with people's anxiety to make themselves understood?

It contains, of course, the rituals generated by that anxiety, as music contains sound. Marianne Moore's poems deal with those rituals as music dealt with them before the clavichord's mathematic was supplanted by the throb of the violin. She will not imitate the rising throbbing curve of emotion, but impede it and quick-freeze it. One impediment is the grid of counted formalisms. Another is the heavy system of nouns:

THE FISH

wade
through black jade. . . .

The black jade got onto the page by the same processes as Ruskin's arms, shields and hills, but without the syntactic lubricants that slide us past a comparison. Simile becomes optical pun, and we have to concentrate on visual likeness amid assault from the strangeness of everything else. "Black jade" (for water) is an optical pun. So are the "ash-heaps" of the "crow-blue mussel-shells." Optical precision brought these ash-heaps and crows into the poem; a moment later it will bring a fan, to swell the bizarre submarine population, and before the poem is over we shall have taken stock of spun glass, turquoise, stars, pink rice-grains, green lilies, toadstools, an iron wedge, a cornice. Each of these optical puns a moment's thought will resolve, yet each such moment interrupts the attention (which does not expect such objects underwater) and interrupts also the expectations of the English sentence, which has two uses for nouns, as doer and as thing done to, "*John* threw the *ball*," and can cope with the odd noun used otherwise ("The dog *treed* the cat"), but loses mobility beneath such a rain of nouns as this poem pours through it, until we are apt to find something odd about so orthodox a usage as "move themselves with *spotlight* swiftness." The sentences are formally impeccable, but their impeccability takes some searching out, interrupted as it so constantly is by its intersections with a different system entirely for displaying nouns.

Just as idiosyncratically the poems deal with quotations. These lie on the page with as arbitrary a look as the nouns wear, set off by quotation marks, yet seldom (never?) familiar quotations: not allusions therefore but found objects, slivers of excellence incorporated into the *assemblage*. One function of the notes to these quotations is to persuade us that they are genuine found objects, not discoveries fabricated by setting quotation marks around phrases of the poet's own devising. The notes are not, like the notes to *The Waste Land*, part of our education; we are not meant to look up the sources; a note to the notes asks that we "take probity on faith" and disregard them. And it is probity, of course, that these poems most obviously enact, creating, within rigorous homemade rules, a crystalline structure, bristling with internal geometry, which (1) exhibits patent optical symmetries; (2) reassures us, if we take the trouble to trace out its syntax, by fulfilling any syntactic law we care to apply; (3) maneuvers through this system, with a maximum of surface discontinuity, some dozens of surprising words and phrases, treated as objects, laid end to end; and (4) justifies each of these objects by a triumphant hidden congruity. The poem is a system, not an utterance, though one can trace an utterance through it.

A thing made, then, not a thing said; and when Williams in the 1920's was working out this distinction, and denominating "the Imagination" as the zone where the poem existed, he had almost no examples to go on but Marianne Moore's. It is hardly too much to say that he arrived at *Spring and All*, and so at the assurances of his own triumphant career, by pondering her 1921 *Poems* (London:

the Egoist Press; the selection was made by "H.D." and [by Mrs. Robert McAlmon, better known as] Bryher). "Marianne's words remain separate," he wrote in *Spring and All*, "each unwilling to group with the others except as they move in one direction." That was something to ponder: they were not caught up in the momentum of a *saying*. And though he admitted that "Her work puzzles me. It is not easy to quote convincingly," still it helped him define his distinction of

prose: statement of facts concerning emotions, intellectual states, data of all sorts . . .

and

poetry: new form dealt with as a reality in itself.

For "the form of poetry is related to the movements of the imagination revealed in words."

The line-ending that does not coincide with a rhetorical pause helps establish the autonomy of the words, "each unwilling to group with the others." They are superbly indifferent, as they move along, to the urgencies of *saying*. And if Williams does not count syllables, or seldom, he divides lines—we have seen him at it—where the voice would not divide them. He does so, that is, after his Jacob's wrestle with the poems of Marianne Moore. In the 1916 "Tract" we find rhetorical line-divisions, later (in the 1917 *All Que Quiere!*) modified into a system of medial spaces:

> *I will teach you   my townspeople*
> *how to perform   a funeral—*
> *for you have it   over a troop*
> *of artists—*
> *unless one should   scour the world—*
> *you have the ground sense   necessary. . . .*

But post-Moore ("At the Faucet of June," 1923) we find,

> *The sunlight in a*
> *yellow plaque upon the*
> *varnished floor*

> *is full of a song*
> *inflated to*
> *fifty pounds pressure*
>
> *at the faucet of*
> *June that rings*
> *the triangle of the air*
>
> *pulling at the*
> *anemones in*
> *Persephone's cow pasture— . . .*

which neither observes the voice's way of pausing nor has anything particularly sensible to offer us upon the plane of *saying*.

The poem is *other* than an utterance: other than what the poet "has to say." Williams often contrived, as Miss Moore did not, that this fact should be underlined by leading the syntactic line through nonsense, while the Imagination reaped its harvest of strange groupings. Miss Moore preferred to double the otherness by setting within the poem some autonomous envelope of energies, a fish, a cat, a ballplayer, to which the poem could conform its oddly depersonalized system of analogies. This autonomous thing she always represents as fulfilling the laws of its being by minding its own business, which is not ours. It also fulfills laws of the poem's being, serving frequently as a point of departure, left behind. Thus the poem headed "An Octopus" is really "about" a glacier, a glacier that not only exists but behaves, and in a way meant to earn our approbation:

AN OCTOPUS

of ice. Deceptively reserved and flat,
it lies 'in grandeur and in mass'
beneath a sea of shifting snow-dunes;
dots of cyclamen-red and maroon on its clearly defined
pseudo-podia

made of glass that will bend—a much needed invention—
comprising twenty-eight ice-fields from fifty to five hundred
        feet thick,
of unimagined delicacy.
'Picking periwinkles from the cracks'
or killing prey with the concentric crushing rigor of the
        python,
it hovers forward 'spider-fashion
on its arms' misleadingly like lace;
its 'ghostly pallor changing
to the green metallic tinge of an anemone-starred pool'. . . .

The icy octopus has by this time torn up and carried toward
us not only the normal detritus of the landscape but five
separate quotations, being in this respect as "deceptively
reserved" as the poet. And the poem continues to edge forward glacially, picking up and shifting periwinkles, py-
thons, spiders, lace, anemones. In fact, by the time it has
drawn toward its close (having incorporated *inter alia* the
Greek language, Henry James, and numerous citations
from the National Parks Rules and Regulations) it appears
to be discussing its own decorum as much as that of the
glacier-octopus:

Relentless accuracy is the nature of this octopus
with its capacity for fact.
'Creeping slowly as with meditated stealth,
its arms seeming to approach from all directions' . . .

It resembles, in its "capacity for fact," the capacity of the
imaginary garden, in the celebrated example, for real toads.
Marianne Moore's subjects—her fields of preoccupation,
rather—have these two notable characteristics among others,
that they are self-sufficient systems of energy, and that they
can appropriate, without hostility, almost anything that
comes near. They affirm, without saying anything, that "In
This Age of Hard Trying, Nonchalance is Good," and that
"There is a great amount of poetry in unconscious / fastidiousness." They are frequently animals; they feed and sleep

and hunt and play; they are graceful without taking pride in their grace. They exemplify the qualities of the poems in which they are found.

Yes, they do; yes, it is striking, this pervasive singleness (though never obvious: nothing is *obvious* here). The singleness helps explain why she was able to make a revolutionary discovery, perhaps without ever knowing what it was. She resembles Columbus, whose mind was on something other than opening new worlds, and died supposing he had shown how to sail to China. For the language flattened, the language *exhibited*, the language staunchly condensing information while frisking in enjoyment of its release from the obligation to do no more than inform: these are the elements of a twentieth-century American poetic, a pivotal discovery of our age. And it seems to have been Marianne Moore's discovery, for Williams, who also discovered it and extended it beyond the reach of her temperament, seems to have discovered it with the aid of her poems. A woman who was never convinced she was writing poems ("I would hardly call it a poem," she said of "Marriage," and "What I write . . . could only be called poetry because there is no other category in which to put it"); she and a frantically busy physician who kept a typewriter screwed to a hinged leaf of his consulting-room desk, to be banged up into typing position between patients: not "poets," not professionals of the word, save for their passion: they were the inventors of an American poetry. The fact is instructive.

Extracting its instruction, we may begin with her avowed hostility to the poetic. We had better not dismiss this as whimsy; it was heuristic.

"I, too, dislike it," she wrote of something called "Poetry." ("I, too"? In alliance with whom? The public? Well, sensible people, presumably.)

I, too, dislike it.
   Reading it, however, with a perfect contempt for it,
      one discovers in it, after all, a place for the
      genuine.

That is all she finally chose to say about "Poetry," on an otherwise blank page of her 1967 *Complete Poems*, though —sensing perhaps that some buyers might otherwise feel cheated—she offered the "original version" as a two-page footnote. (Had a longish poem ever before been a footnote to a three-line excerpt from itself? She didn't care. The only tradition she acknowledged was that of rectitude. That's instructive, too.)

It wasn't merely her octogenarian conscience that suffered these drastic fits of rectitude. "Poetry" has a long history of being fussed with, and as long ago as 1924, when the author was a merry-eyed 37, a convulsive revision deprived it of fully seventy percent of its words, including the famous ones that stipulate "imaginary gardens with real toads in them." She also expelled "the immovable critic twinkling his skin like a horse that feels a flea," and the counted-syllable grid, and the five-stanza layout. By 1932 a new upheaval had restored the stanzas, but only three of them, arranged on a different grid. The critic was also back, but now "twitching" his skin, and "flea" had been escalated to "fly," but "Poetry" was still gardenless and toadless. Two years later the poem looked pretty much as it had originally, toads, five stanzas and all, with "twitching" retained but "fly" once more "flea," the syllable count of unprecedented elasticity and about midway a whole line missing. This is the so-called "original version" of the 1967 footnote, appended to the most calamitous reworking of all, in which toads, gardens, critic and just about everything else—the baseball fan, the statistician, the bat, even plural elephants— went down the tubes. It's hard not to conclude that her asserted dislike of poetry, nearly the one stable element amid all these upheavals, extended to dislike of words she'd written at 32 and subsequently could neither subdue nor bring herself to discard. However they plagued her, they said something she wanted to say.

She did indeed dislike poetry, she used emphatically to insist. One time, citing

> *No man may him hyde*
> *From Deth holow-eyed,*

she made a little inventory of dislikes:

I dislike the reversed order of words; don't like to be impeded by an unnecessary capital at the beginning of every line; I don't like, here, the meaning; the cadence coming close to being the sole reason for all that follows, the accent on "holow" rather than on "eyed," so firmly placed that the most willful reader cannot misplace it. . . .

This is to reject, well, very much. If more careful in its discriminations than Williams' shoving aside of "Europe—the past," it has a comparable thrust. Nevertheless, reading poetry without enchantment, "one discovers in it, after all, a place for the genuine": a place, as she went on to say in 1919, for "real toads." That's what poetry is, a place; not a deed but a location. "A kind of collection of flies in amber," Miss Moore was to call her own poetry, "if not a cabinet of fossils."

This attitude rejects historical nostalgia. When Dr. Johnson wrote their Lives, "the Poets" were all nearly contemporaneous: men alive so recently that everyone understood the world nearly as they did. We may guess that Miss Moore would have been at home in that climate, when a poem collected concentrations of acknowledged wisdom, and felicities of expression were prized and borrowed. Expulsion from such a paradise occurred, however, soon afterward, when historical consciousness was engrossing poets and poetry began to feed on its own past, finding delicious succulence in words like "faery":

> *. . . The same that oft-times hath*
> *Charm'd magic casements, opening on the foam*
> *Of perilous seas, in faery lands forlorn.*

Keats's poem calls itself an "Ode," an historical ritual. By mid-century it seemed part of the office of art to incorporate the contemporary into history. Into an evocation of romantic departure, already ritualized by 1866, the young Mallarmé inserted the word "Steamer" (an English word, moreover):

> Je partirai! Steamer balançant ta mâture,
> Lève l'ancre pour une exotique nature!

At just about the same time, Manet painted two Parisian dandies, one of them his own brother and both in the studio dress of that day, at the center of an iconography paraphrased from Giorgione. When the fuss had died down after several decades, it became clear that *Le Déjeuner sur l'Herbe* was a bland incorporation of the Present into Art History, into the artifice of eternity. Its visual idiom, quoting Giorgione, declines to view a bohemian picnic as if through contemporary eyes. In much the same way Eliot, quoting the idiom of Tennyson, declines to render Prufrock's social malaise empirically—

> *There will be time to murder and create,*
> *And time for all the works and days of hands*
> *That lift and drop a question on your plate . . .*

—moving his subject into the domain occupied by "Poetry," by verbal rituals historically sanctioned. We can tell that "Prufrock" sounds like Poetry before we can tell what realities it engages with. And Eliot's work infuriated Williams (though not Miss Moore, who admired its aplomb).

Miss Moore's modest effort was not to deflect "poetry" or to destroy it, but to ignore it: that is to say, ignore its rituals. She made up difficult rules of her own, some of which as they evolved remained in force (end-stopped lines for choice, and after 1929, rhyme), while others—the specific syllable grid, the density and audibility of the rhymes—

hold good only for the duration of the poem in hand. It's a homemade art, like the sampler wrought in cross-stitch. Sometimes it will allow the conjunction between rule and theme to appear almost naïvely, as though a principle known to Homer or Donne had just been improvised. A rapid alternation of sounds in "Light is Speech" was suggested by the winking of a lighthouse—*

> One can say more of sunlight
>   than of speech; but speech
>   and light, each
> aiding each . . .

and the assertion that the Jerboa moves

> By fifths and sevenths,
> in leaps of two lengths

is encompassed in a stanza that opens with five syllables per line and closes with seven. But the primary function of rule is not to look jauntily appropriate but to intercept the flow of phrasing, and make us pause, pause, pause, on the single words:

> By fifths and sevenths,
> in leaps of two lengths,
>   like the uneven notes
>   of the Bedouin flute, it stops its gleaming
>   on little wheel-castors, and makes fern-seed
>   foot-prints with kangaroo speed.
>
> Its leaps should be set
> to the flageolet;
>   pillar body erect
>   on a three-cornered smooth-working Chippendale
>   claw—propped on hind legs, and tail as third toe,
>   between leaps to its burrow.

—as usual a thick system of seeming nouns, many of which turn out to be adjectival, each one an act of attention, and the Gestalt *exhibited* with superb indifference to literary

* According to a reminiscence of the late Lester Littlefield's.

history. The single words are stripped of history, "pillar" of classical associations, "Chippendale" of antique ones. Word by word, we must take the point, and let historical overtones go. One cannot call the verse formless; one cannot succumb, either, to unreflective ritual enjoyment, caressed by sounds. Attention, attention, that is the injunction, as it was Thoreau's injunction. Averting attention we can follow nothing, neither the structure of a sentence nor the applicability of a phrase. Through cluttered tidiness, the reader must move like a cat.

And feeding into this verse, nourishing it, tumbles a richness of found phrases: not, however, the "pleasing wraiths of former masteries" that Dr. Williams discerned enhancing the words of traditional poetry, but simply the accuracies of people who have observed something interesting. Thus "New York" gleaned a comparison of the fawn's spots to satin needlework from the *Literary Digest*, a snobbish vaunt from a book about *The Psychology of Dress*, and a terminal phrase, "accessibility to experience," from James. The effect of such a procedure is to democratize "tradition" very considerably; anyone may enrich tradition if he will just keep his mind on his subject. Leafing the Notes, one is struck by the near absence of phrases gleaned from poets, by the scarcity in general of "literary" names, and by the high concentration of magazine writers. The *Illustrated London News* is much drawn on; writers were likely to suit Marianne Moore's purposes when they had pictures nearby to keep them honest. The notes to "Nine Nectarines" preserve a citation from an auction catalogue (though, oddly enough, the part of the poem to which it refers was deleted before 1951) and the notes to "Four Quartz Crystal Clocks" call a Bell Telephone technical leaflet to our attention: such writings bespeak a minute obligation to fact.

She chose all the snippets for a single reason: she admired the phrasing. Her longest poem, "Marriage," she later described simply as "statements that took my fancy which I tried to arrange plausibly." In *Observations*, extending this principle, she even supplied an amusing Index to the things the poems try to arrange plausibly; among the C's we find,

> *chipmunk, nine-striped, 85*
> CHOOSING, PICKING AND, 55, 97
> *Christ on Parnassus, 102*
> *chrysalis, 57, 98*
> *cigars, 57*
> *circular traditions, 75, 102*
> *circus, 107*
> *clay pots, 28*
> *coach, gilt, 65; wheel yellow, 35*
> *cockatrices, 71, 101*
> *cockroaches, 57*
> *coffin, 79, 104*
> *Coliseum, 63*

She even gleaned found objects from the likes of editorial pages, addressing a Rose through polysyllabic clichés:

*You do not seem to realize that beauty is a liability rather than
an asset—that in view of the fact that spirit creates form we
are justified in supposing
that you must have brains. . . .*

This brought to Eliot's delighted mind the vision of "a whole people playing uncomfortably at clenches and clevelandisms," but Miss Moore, whose conscience was her admirers' despair, later disliked the poem (perhaps as disrespectful to its materials?) and banished it.

That suppressed poem ("Roses Only") chattered with the voices of others, molded into a single voice which became the poet's somewhat alarming, notably tart *persona*. It is yet one more instructive episode: speech not her own became a means of satire, and was itself satirized. She was uncomfortable with satire, and the poem, which dates from 1917, was deleted from every collection after 1935. In what continued to be reprinted we hear one voice only, hers, sharp and economical at first, in later years fussily generous. Such a sequence as

> ... *Émile Littré,*
> *philology's determined,*
> *ardent eight-volume*
>   *Hippocrates-charmed*
> *editor. A*
> *man on fire, a scientist of*
> *freedoms, was firm Maximilien*
>
> *Paul Émile Littré. . . .*

tells us remarkably little while nodding its head in vehement approbation. And it takes up one fifth of its poem. (The note is more economical: "Littré [1801–81] devoted the years 1839–62 to translating and editing Hippocrates.") Contrast the speed, eighteen years earlier, of the lines on Adam—

> *Unnerved by the nightingale*
> *and dazzled by the apple,*
> *impelled by 'the illusion of a fire*
> *effectual to extinguish fire',*
> *compared with which*
> *the shining of the earth*
> *is but deformity—a fire*
> *'as high as deep*
> *as bright as broad*
> *as long as life itself',*
> *he stumbles over marriage,*
> *'a very trivial object indeed'*
> *to have destroyed the attitude*
> *in which he stood—*
> *the ease of the philosopher*
> *unfathered by a woman. . . .*

—and consider the damage done to the poetry by a sensed obligation to be respectful.

Like Stevens', hers is a poetry for one voice; like Stevens', it works by surface complication, with little variety of feeling. Unlike Stevens', it has no traffic—has never had any at all—with the cadences of the Grand Style, with Tradition, but works by a principle exclusively its own, the witty transit through minute predilections. Unlike Stevens' poetry, finally, hers deteriorates, as it were, through insufficient grasp of its own principles. Having been held together by a temperament, it grows dilute as the temperament grows more accommodating. And yet it is a turning point, as Stevens' is not. When American verse was looking for a way to cope with the perceived world's multifarious otherness, it was Marianne Moore's best work that was decisive.

Causing her best poems to enact with such rigor the moral virtues they celebrate, Miss Moore skirted the tradition of the dandy, whose life was a controlled thing and whose norms of conduct were stylistic. Dandyism's principal modern celebrant was Ernest Hemingway, whose bullfights and lion-hunts were aesthetic gestures and whose descriptions of clear water running over stones were moral achievements. It was Hemingway in our time who fulfilled most dramatically Ruskin's precept that to see something, and tell what one saw in a plain way, is "poetry, prophecy and religion all in one," though the second term would have made Hemingway uneasy. We may see in his career one apotheosis to which the discipline of describing natural objects was tending during many decades.

But Hemingway's conception of style as the criterion of life contains one element totally alien to any poetic effect of Marianne Moore's: *self-appreciation.* To take satisfaction in one's achievements, and to undertake like achievements in quest of more of that satisfaction—this is the dual temptation by which such a poetic is beset; and the theme of many poems of Miss Moore is precisely the duty to resist it. Her black elephant utters an opening vaunt not immune from self-congratulation:

> *Openly, yes,*
> *with the naturalness*
> > *of the hippopotamus or the alligator*
> > *when it climbs out on the bank to experience the*
>
> *sun, I do these*
> *things which I do, which please*
> > *no one but myself . . .*

but midway through the poem a crucial discrimination is made:

> *. . . nevertheless I*
> > *perceive feats of strength to be inexplicable after*
> > *all; and I am on my guard; external poise, it*
>
> *has its centre*
> *well nurtured—we know*
> > *where—in pride; but spiritual poise, it has its centre where?*

To offer behavior which is "inexplicable after all" is to take no credit for it. The "beautiful element of unreason" has its uses. Another poem recommends "unconscious fastidiousness," and having surveyed with some astringency the behavior of a swan and of an ant, asks,

> *. . . What is*
> *there in being able*
> > *to say that one has dominated the stream in an attitude of*
> > > *self-defence;*
> > *in proving that one has had the experience*
> > *of carrying a stick?*

—For that matter, of fighting a bull? To "prove that one has had the experience" of playing with a cat, or seeing a fish, or pretending to be an elephant, is just what a poetic of visual experience is likely to find itself engaged upon, even as Ruskin tended to be intent on proving that he alone had ever really seen a fir tree. In the same way, much fine photography stirs feelings closer to envy than to delight: "The man who held the camera was *here*," it tends to say, "and moreover at this unique moment; do you not wish you had been here, too?"

Some of the formal obstacles Marianne Moore laid across the assertions of her sentences were to help her avoid seeming to imply that a cat or a fish has never really been looked at before. Their presence raises, however, a further problem: how to avoid asserting that one has had the dexterity to overcome formal obstacles. It is here that her preoccupation with otherness helps.

For those autonomous envelopes of energy she so admired are *other*, as Nature for Wordsworth never was. Where Hemingway imitated bullfighters, she was content to admire ballplayers. Her cats, pangolins, jerboas, elephants are not beings she half-perceives and half-creates. Their accomplishments are wholly their own. It is not the poet who notes that the jerboa is sand-colored, but the jerboa that "honours the sand by assuming its colour." Similarly, it is the jerboa that has discovered a flute rhythm for itself, "by fifths and sevenths, / in leaps of two lengths," and to play the flageolet in its presence is not our ingenuity but our obligation. "Its leaps should be set / to the flageolet." So when, as normally, we find that the poem is itself enacting the virtues it discerns in its subject, we are not to say that it is commenting on its own aesthetic, as in Hemingway's celebrations of the way one works close to the bull; rather that its aesthetic is an offering to the virtuosity of the brisk little creature that changes pace so deftly, and direction so deftly, and keeps intent, and keeps alert, and both offers and refrains from flaunting its agility.

This works best with animals, because they don't know their own virtuosity, and with athletes because at decisive moments they haven't time for self-appreciation, there being a ball to catch that won't wait. ("I could of caught it with a pair of pliers," said the exuberant outfielder, but that was afterward.) That is why Miss Moore's best poems are unpeopled save by glimpsed exemplars of verbal or synaptic dexterity. It is also why, as she admitted to her system other people's values, a poetic misfortune for which her sense of wartime obligations may be in part blamed, she relaxed and blurred her normal deftness and neatness, aware of the inappropriateness of seeming crisp. To be crisp even in praise of people's excellence is to make oneself a little the proprietor of their virtue; one senses that she sensed that to be improper.

At her best, she was other from us, and her subjects other from her, and saying with the elephant, "I do these / things which I do, which please / no one but myself," she was fulfilling a nature of her own. For the unclubbable cat she had offered this defense:

> *As for the disposition*
> *invariably to affront, an animal with claws wants to have to use*
> *them; that eel-like extension of trunk into tail is not an*
> *accident. To*
> *leap, to lengthen out, divide the air—to purloin, to pursue.*
> *To tell the hen: fly over the fence, go in the wrong way in*
> *your perturbation—this is life; to do less would be*
> *nothing but dishonesty.*

And a being with an eye wants to have to use it, and a being with a typewriter, and a being with a memory. So by a long way round, by way of a poetic that dislocates, seemingly, each nuance of normal utterance, this rendition of the experience of the eye came to seem natural after all, an instance of commendable behavior. It was a limited, remarkable achievement. It imitates without congratulating itself on having thought to imitate, or on having found the means. It compels our minds to move across an opaque and resistant surface, that of the printed language, in emulation of the eye's experience moving across the contours of a pangolin's armor; and it impedes the facilities of the conclusion drawn, the thing said, the instance appropriated into a moral system, on the principle that while psychic experience flows naturally into utterance, optical experience must be carefully anatomized before we can too readily allow it to be psychic. For the supreme insult—this is its final claim— the supreme insult to that which is other than we, that which, perceived by the eye, is *therefore* other: the supreme insult we can offer to the other is to have, on too little acquaintance, something to say "about" it.

V ᜡ Small Ritual Truths

"I'm not joking you [said the count]. I never joke people. Joke people and you make enemies. That's what I always say."

And the count and Brett, with Jake the Joke in attendance, proceed to toss phrases back and forth like juggler's balls, the routine as stylized as a song and dance, or as a Gilbert and Sullivan duet:

"You're right," Brett said. "You're terribly right. I always joke people and I haven't a friend in the world. Except Jake here."

"You don't joke him."

"That's it."

"Do you, now?" asked the count. "Do you joke him?"

Brett looked at me and wrinkled up the corners of her eyes.

"No," she said. "I wouldn't joke him."

"See," said the count. "You don't joke him."

"This is a hell of a dull talk," Brett said. "How about some of that champagne?"

—*The Sun Also Rises*, by Ernest Hemingway, page 58; with which compare:

> DUSTY: *How about Pereira?*
> DORIS: *What about Pereira?*
>   *I don't care.*
> DUSTY: *You don't care!*
>   *Who pays the rent?*
> DORIS: *Yes he pays the rent*
> DUSTY: *Well some men don't and some men do*
>   *Some men don't and you know who*
> DORIS: *You can have Pereira*
> DUSTY: *What about Pereira?*
> DORIS: *He's no gentleman, Pereira:*
>   *You can't trust him!*
> DUSTY: *Well that's true*

—"Fragment of a Prologue," by T. S. Eliot, first published in *The Criterion* for October 1926. Hemingway's novel was published in the same month.

Since there is no possibility of interaction, we have here another instance of Eliot's uncanny radar, which had also elicited from the dark of the twenties that symbol of brooding eyes above a plain of death—

> *The eyes are not here*
> *There are no eyes here*
> *In this valley of dying stars*
> *In this hollow valley*
> *This broken jaw of our lost kingdoms*

—so similar to Scott Fitzgerald's most famous symbol, "the eyes of Dr. T. J. Eckleburg," "blue and gigantic," which "look out of no face" across the "valley of ashes" where men "move dimly and already crumbling through the powdery air," that it would be difficult not to believe that one passage suggested the other were it not again for the nearly synchronous publication.

Eliot's verse of the twenties, though there is relatively little of it, reads like a compendium of a decade's symbols;

no other twentieth-century decade has yielded in that way to being summed up by images. To encounter comparable images, comparable expressive mannerisms, in the fictions of Fitzgerald and Hemingway is to be reminded to what extent these two expatriates were engaged in an enterprise like the expatriate poet's. All three had encounters—Eliot and Fitzgerald tangential, Hemingway repeated and fructifying—with the most programmatic of expatriates and the most stubborn, Gertrude Stein, who never ceased to affirm that her preoccupation (in Paris) was with America, "the oldest country in the world," she would say, "because it has been living in the twentieth century longer than any other country"—by which she meant, ever since the Civil War. They made Civil War rifles from interchangeable parts, and moved troops around by railroad, and Sherman invented "total war," and the North and the South became bitter geographical abstractions. Miss Stein made paragraphs out of die-cut parts:

This one, and the one I am now beginning describing is Martha Hersland and this is a little story of the acting in her of her being in her very young living, this one was a very little one then and she was running and she was in the street and it was a muddy one and she had an umbrella that she was dragging and she was crying. "I will throw the umbrella in the mud," she was saying, she was very little then, she was just beginning her schooling, "I will throw the umbrella in the mud," she said and no one was near her and she was dragging the umbrella and bitterness possessed her, "I will throw the umbrella in the mud," she was saying and nobody heard her, the others had run ahead to get home and they had left her, "I will throw the umbrella in the mud," and there was desperate anger in her; "I have throwed the umbrella in the mud," burst from her, she had thrown the umbrella in the mud and that was the end of it all in her. She had thrown the umbrella in the mud and no one heard her as it burst from her, "I have throwed the umbrella in the mud," it was the end of all that to her.

Flaubert would have written this differently, but not better.

Differently, in that he would have seen the incident differently, not as a discharge of baffled energy but as an instance of Martha's early petulance, significant to the analyst. Not better, because what is there to improve? It lies on the page, a rectangular perfection, elements cycling and thrusting like connecting rods. It might be a detail in a design for a prose locomotive. Its monotony is electric, like Morse Code. Pressed flat into ritual symmetries, that was how Miss Stein intuited twentieth-century language; and when she told Hemingway that remarks were not literature, she was enjoining him not to let a sentence escape from the system, and acquire a trajectory, and claim to be "about" something. She was the Mondriaan of prose, and her intuitions were often profound, even as her prose was often unreadable. Her prose was resisting a drag toward lyric nostalgia. In his litany of the comers to Gatsby's parties, which begins ". . . the names of those who came to Gatsby's house that summer" and ends, "All these people came to Gatsby's house in the summer," Scott Fitzgerald interpolates, after "the Kellehers and the Dewars and the Scullys and S. W. Belcher and the Smirkes and the young Quinns," a lyric episode:

Benny McClenahan arrived always with four girls. They were never quite the same ones in physical person, but they were so identical one with another that it inevitably seemed they had been there before. I have forgotten their names— Jacqueline, I think, or else Consuela, or Gloria or Judy or June, and their last names were either the melodious names of flowers and months or the sterner ones of the great American capitalists whose cousins, if pressed, they would confess themselves to be.

This might be a paraphrase, rather quickly written, of a text by Gertrude Stein, insatiable quester of dulcet interchangeabilities, Jacqueline or Consuela, Gloria or Judy or June, and flowers, ah, and flowers.

A prose that should be as absolute as paint, that was a dream of the twenties; and likewise a verse that should be as spare as such a prose. It was a decade of Writing, a craft with a mystique; and what the writer got down "truly"— Hemingway's signature is on that adverb—would last: which means, it would turn into a symbol.

"I was trying to write then," he later recalled of, say, 1922, "and I found the greatest difficulty . . . was to put down what really happened in action; what the actual things were which produced the emotion that you experienced." This, if you could set it down, would be "the real thing, the sequence of motion and fact which made the emotion and which would be as valid in a year or ten years or, with luck and if you stated it purely enough, always."

"The sequence of motion and fact which made the emotion" is apparently rephrased from certain words of Eliot's: "a set of objects, a situation, a chain of events which shall be the formula of that *particular* emotion." Eliot set down these words late in 1919, reviewing a book about *Hamlet*. Late in 1920 they were incorporated in *The Sacred Wood*, and complete with an encapsulating phrase, "objective correlative," they lodged very quickly in many receptive minds.

The only way of expressing emotion in the form of art is by finding an "objective correlative"; in other words, a set of objects, a situation, a chain of events which shall be the formula of that *particular* emotion; such that when the external facts, which must terminate in sensory experience, are given, the emotion is immediately released.

Eliot was trying to explain to his own satisfaction why the rhetorical set-pieces in *Hamlet* seem applicable to the cosmos is general, and may even plausibly be redistributed through the play when it is arranged for acting. The reason seemed to be that the sequence of events in *Hamlet* did not formulate clear emotions capable of releasing just these soliloquies at just these moments. By contrast, he thought, Macbeth's "Tomorrow and tomorrow and tomorrow . . ." comes just where it does, and can come nowhere else, and does not impress us as a fine interpolation, because the sequence of events in *Macbeth* culminates at that point ("The Queen, my Lord, is dead") in just that hollow oaken estimate of life as an idiot's tale full of sound and fury. But in *Hamlet* Shakespeare is trying to *tell* us, by way of the soliloquies, what we should feel at this or that moment; even so, Hemingway asserted, a man writing in a hurry for a newspaper "with one trick and another"—he knew those tricks—"communicated the emotion aided by an element of timeliness which gives a certain emotion to any account of something that has happened on that day." "But the real thing"—?

Before the waiter brought the sherry the rocket that announced the fiesta went up in the square. It burst and there was a gray ball of smoke high up above the Theatre Gayarre, across on the other side of the plaza. The ball of smoke hung in the sky like a shrapnel burst, and as I watched, another rocket came up to it, trickling smoke in the bright sunlight. I saw the bright flash as it burst and another little cloud of smoke appeared. By the time the second rocket had burst there were so many people in the arcade, that had been empty a moment before, that the waiter, holding the bottle high up over his head, could hardly get through the crowd to our table. People were coming into the square from all sides, and down the street we heard the pipes and the fifes and the drums coming. They were playing the *riau-riau* music, the pipes shrill and the drums pounding, and behind them came the men and boys dancing. . . .

"What really happened, what the actual things were": attention on sherry, interrupted by one rocket which carries the eye away from our table to the sky above the other side of the plaza; the scale of perception is enlarging. Then another rocket, "trickling smoke in the bright sunlight"; and as the eye drops (to track a possible third?) the arcade in which we sit proves suddenly crowded (the sherry bottle bobbing toward us above the crowd), while from other such arcades likewise the vast space across which we were looking is suddenly filling with people. Then music sounding, then behind the musicians the men and boys dancing. . . . The impact of thousands of people turning festive could not be more economically conveyed: and in level declarative sentences, with nowhere an exclamation point. ("The noise! And the crowds!" said an officer trying to describe Dunkirk without having found his objective correlative.) As for the sudden compaction of the crowd, the progress of the sherry bottle conveys it: ". . . there were so many people in the arcade, that had been empty a minute before, that the waiter, holding the bottle high up over his head, could hardly get through the crowd to our table." And single words are sequenced likewise: the bottle is held high up over his head; to delete that "up" is to delete an instability, kinesthetic because rhythmic, and to lend that bottle's progress a misleading Newtonian stateliness.

Looking more coldly, one might reduce this to a bag of tricks: the trick, for instance, of taking our attention away from the arcade while the crowd fills it, so as to avoid cluttered sentences about people appearing; or the trick of deafening us with *riau-riau* music so as not to pause over description of the musicians. ". . . The pipes shrill and the drums pounding, and behind them came the men and boys dancing": behind an "and," the musicians have entered the square, unseen.

But the economical doing of anything will look like a sequence of tricks if we retrace it slowly. If, having tied a bowline by tracing the diagram, we watch an expert tie it with just two gestures, we may be tempted to say he has employed a trick with his middle finger; whereas he simply understands the knot. Still, one can catch Hemingway employing tricks:

> He watched the sky lightening beyond the long point of marsh, and turning in the sunken barrel, he looked out across the frozen lagoon, and the marsh, and saw the snow-covered mountains a long way off. Low as he was, no foothills showed, and the mountains rose abruptly from the plain. As he looked toward the mountains he could feel a breeze on his face and he knew, then, the wind would come from there, rising with the sun, and that some birds would surely come flying in from the sea when the wind disturbed them.

This is not "what really happened" but a paraphrase. Twice Hemingway talks to the reader, interpolating "low as he was" to explain why no foothills showed, and gathering some clauses around the phrase "he knew" to explain the hunter's expectation of birds. Six "and's" meanwhile give that texture of authenticity, sensation following sensation, by which we are meant to be assured that nothing analytic is being smuggled in, and the nouns denote primary natural phenomena, lightening sky, frozen lagoon, snow-covered mountains: objective correlatives, we are lulled into conceding, of primary emotions. The tired Hemingway of *Across the River and Into the Trees* (two primary nouns; an "and") had composed so many sentences around primary nouns that he no longer noticed when he was cheating.

One might distinguish between these two examples in another way, by noticing that the fiesta passage, rockets, sherry bottle, crowd, music, dancers, would be intelligible and exciting in a sequence of movie shots, whereas the duck-blind passage transposed to cinema would convey no assurance that birds will surely come flying even if in some ultimate nickelodeon a breeze could be blown on the spectator's face. The doctrine of the "objective correlative" is dramatic and finally cinematic in principle. We should not be surprised that Eliot arrived at it in pondering the defective working of a play, and cinema is the ultimate case. Plays can cheat with language, soliloquies, verbal incitements. The cinema of 1923, with no dialogue, cannot cheat at all, except by relying on a primitive fascination with motion pictures to carry the viewer across emotional dropouts.

For it was just as the narrative art reached one kind of theoretical purity that the motion picture began to supersede it. During some two generations a complex of criteria, some aesthetic, some moral, some metaphysical, had been urging the writer toward an ideal of showing, not telling, as though toward the obligations of a new medium, not envisaged in Flaubert's lifetime, which should not be capable of any procedure but showing. Hemingway's best writing now seems as "classical" and as old-fashioned as the silent film it intimately resembles. In the same way Gertrude Stein, one of whose plays begins

> *Six.*
> *Twenty.*
> *Outrageous.*

might have conceived a script for Buster Keaton, whose immobile face traces a cycloid curve across the screen as he sits on the connecting rod of his Civil War locomotive. Miss Stein might have, and Samuel Beckett did, and the art of all three writers, Hemingway's notably, was the art of avoiding subtitles. It is with the title that the silent film cheats. Keaton in *The General* has nearly none, except the ones that tell us which moving masses of men are Union, which Confederate, making up for the inability of monochrome film to distinguish blue from gray. Griffith in his portentous pot-boiler *Way Down East* had dozens, hundreds. They made it more like "literature."

In the 1920's the most pertinent influence on the narrative art was surely the reading public's newest habit: it was starting to go to the movies. This was to mean, eventually, the obsolescence of a whole order of fiction, of the kind that the *Post* and *Collier's* and *Scribner's* once bought at seller's-market prices from Ernest Hemingway and Scott Fitzgerald and John Dos Passos and Sherwood Anderson and Booth Tarkington and Janet Ayer Fairbank and Mary Roberts Rinehart and other men with two names and women with three. Television, the successor to the movie-going habit, now gratifies the appetite such fiction once gratified, and few magazines buy stories any longer (and the *Post* and *Collier's* and *Scribner's* have all vanished). The short story is now what Hemingway tried to make it and also what all obsolete conventions are, an art form.

More pertinently, movies taught audiences a new vocabulary, that of the sensuous image, moving boats, wind rippling water, leaves swaying, so that when the writer crisply described such matters he was understood not to be supplying a "setting" but advancing his action as surely as by a conversation or a gunshot; and taught them a new grammar, that of juxtaposed shots, so that the writer could switch attention rapidly without having to say that he would now pause to take up another thread; and a new syntax likewise, of event counterpointed with setting, or dialogue with action, so that what Kenneth Burke was to call "perspective by incongruity" ceased to be a property of metaphysical poems and other historical curiosities. Film invented none of these devices, which may all be illustrated from Flaubert, but film disseminated them, so that writers could employ them less self-consciously. That is one reason many books once thought difficult now do not intimidate even sophomores who do not read very much; we find *Ulysses* selling copiously in paperback without benefit even of the convention that it is "outspoken."

The movies, which began by entrancing folk on hard benches with the simple illusion of motion—a train pulling into a station, a horse-drawn fire truck a-gallop, the chutes at Coney Island—stumbled into the aesthetic of the objective correlative as soon as they began trying to tell stories. The titles, for a while, did the narrating, with visual sequences interpolated; but titles were soon a nuisance to be eliminated so far as feasible. The distinction between showing and telling could scarcely have been encountered on a more practical plane.

Movies have another characteristic pertinent to the writer's concerns: they contain no descriptions. All the details a writer must itemize, all the visual relationships he must specify, the characteristics of mood and light he must nuance with such effort, the camera blots up instantly. Environments are simply *there*. So are personal mannerisms, ways of holding a cigarette or a teacup, plays of human expression, details of hair, of dress, of stature, of muscled vigor or coy allure. So the director need do none of the things Theodore Dreiser felt he had to do (1911), in the course of getting Jennie Gerhardt and her mother located and specified: need not describe the hotel where they seek work—

. . . The lobby was large and had been recently redecorated. Both floor and wainscot were of white marble, kept shiny by frequent polishing. There was an imposing staircase with handrails of walnut and toestrips of brass. . . . [85 more words of this]—

and need not describe the women—

She was of a helpless, fleshy build, with a frank, open countenance and an innocent, diffident manner. Her eyes were large and patient, and in them dwelt such a shadow of distress as only those who have looked sympathetically into the countenances of the distraught and helpless poor know anything about. Anyone could see where the daughter behind her got the timidity and shamefacedness which now caused her to stand back and look indifferently away. . . .

Various people, it is true, the set decorator, the costumier, the casting director, must see to all these details, but no one need be at the trouble of arranging them serially into sentences for serial absorption. Once they are present, the camera will snap them up instantly, and the spectator will absorb them peripherally as he watches the action unfold.

Hemingway, like the camera, gives us peripheral detail as the action unfolds:

> In the white water at the foot of the dam it was deep. As I baited up, a trout shot up out of the white water into the falls and was carried down. Before I could finish baiting, another trout jumped at the falls, making the same lovely arc and disappearing into the water that was thundering down. I put on a good-sized sinker and dropped into the white water close to the edge of the timbers of the dam.

There is no separate description of the falls, the pool, the dam. Simple nouns convey these elements as the narrative needs them.

Which is not to say that Hemingway (1925) has been "influenced" by cinema, or that Eliot (1919) had its exactions in mind when he formulated the doctrine of the "objective correlative." Since Stendhal and Flaubert, prose narrative had been tending toward such criteria. We need only note that they are asymptotic to the criteria of the cinema, so that a film-trained audience finds such writing less unfamiliar than a readership educated by Walter Scott and Theodore Dreiser. Similarly, when Conrad Aiken, praising *Gatsby*'s "excellence of form" while it was still a new book, detected a considerable debt to "the influence of the cinema," he was quick to note parallels also with Henry James: "a peculiar conjunction, but not so peculiar if one reflects on the flash-backs and close-ups and paralleled themes of that 'little experiment in the style of Gyp,' *The Awkward Age*."

It is easy to detect "the influence of the cinema" as the first principal character in *The Great Gatsby* is hunted down by the narrator's eye:

. . . Their house was even more elaborate than I had expected, a cheerful red-and-white Georgian Colonial mansion, overlooking the bay. The lawn started at the beach and ran toward the front door for a quarter of a mile, jumping over sun-dials and brick walls and burning gardens—finally when it reached the house drifting up the side in bright vines as though from the momentum of its run. The front was broken by a line of French windows, glowing now with reflected gold and wide open to the warm windy afternoon, and Tom Buchanan in riding clothes was standing with his legs apart on the front porch.

Yet when Fitzgerald arranges our impressions in that order we need not say either that he has anticipated the zoom, or that he has studied the earlier convention of long shot, medium shot and close-up, but simply that he is reflecting in a relatively light novel the procedures Flaubert and Conrad had evolved with decades of effort, to float and maneuver their fictional dreadnoughts. The too-elaborate house is not "setting," it is a first adumbration of the values by which the Buchanans live, just as the first house the Bovarys inhabit adumbrates, with its too-large clock on the exiguous mantel and its plaster curé in the miserable back garden, a former wife's thwarted yearning after elegance. Fitzgerald's acute sensitivity to the things people did with their money afforded him an economical way of delineating their values, summing up, in an inventory of surroundings which is actually an inventory of purchases, a hundred revealing things they have done before they did what they are doing now.

So natural to him was this way of thinking that it is difficult to say how much he may have learned from such a predecessor as Flaubert. The hermit of Croisset had to beat up by sheer will-power an interest in purchases he would have had no desire to make for himself, and décor he would not have been caught dead arranging, and when, on the first page of *Un Coeur Simple*, we read of that dismal, unforgettable parlor with its eight white chairs lined up along the paneled wall, its pyramid of boxes arranged on the piano, and its clock in the form of a Temple of Vesta, we sense behind the neatly dovetailed sentences the powerful negative emotions that compacted them. But Gatsby's car—ah, Gatsby's car, how Scott Fitzgerald would have loved to own Gatsby's car!—So much so that it was as easy for him to write the forty words that elevate it into symbolhood as it was to slip in the two spoilsport adjectives that denote his narrator's resistance to such gauds.

Vectors are converging here. Detail guided by the writer's daydreams is serving on the printed page to register the things his people do with their opportunities; and this, considered as a literary procedure, is congruent with Flaubert's way of fixing to his pages his French bourgeoisie, and also with the cinematic aesthetic that makes its points by way of what we are shown. Cinema in turn, as it happened, was to grow preoccupied with moneyed daydreams, mindlessly so. Fitzgerald could be naïve but was never mindless.

Nor ever, as it happens, self-conscious (however expert) about the efficient literary methods *Gatsby* employs so casually. What he was apt to be self-conscious about was phrasemaking: the *sententiae* of Nick Carraway, or the rampant lusciousness with which he festooned the moment when Gatsby's heart beat faster as Daisy's white face came nearer:

> He knew that when he kissed this girl, and forever wed his unutterable visions to her perishable breath, his mind would never romp again like the mind of God. So he waited, listening for a moment longer to the tuning-fork that had been struck upon a star. Then he kissed her. At his lips' touch she blossomed for him like a flower and the incarnation was complete.

Though we hear instantly of Gatsby's "appalling sentimentality," it is difficult to be persuaded that these sentences were composed so we might find them appalling. We are meant to admire them. They are Fine Writing, of a piece with Nick's unripe evocation of "the abortive sorrows and short-winded elations of men." Just sufficiently justified by Gatsby's pretentiousness, just sufficiently rebuked by the narrator's disdain, they leave their flavor of chocolate cream on the page without hopelessly smearing the novel, testimony (since we have been invoking Flaubert) to a touch of provinciality inherent in Scott Fitzgerald's accomplishment.

Hemingway too had his provinciality. He wanted to be admired for the things he knew, things not known in Oak Park, Ill., and his method, requiring as it did the introduction of so much specified fact, frequently permitted the indulgence of this desire.

> We turned off the Avenue up the Rue des Pyramides, through the traffic of the Rue de Rivoli, and through a dark gate into the Tuileries. She cuddled against me and I put my arm around her. . . .

This remembers the cab ride in *Madame Bovary*, which went up and down so many specified streets and past so many landmarks, the driver whipping, the cab shaking, the seduction (to the horror of Flaubert's contemporaries) proceeding unseen, shake and jiggle and bounce. It remembers the *Bovary* ride in ironic miniature—just a few streets, and the girl is a whore, and Jake is impotent—and while it is doing that, it also remembers to let us know that somebody here (Jake Barnes? Ernest Hemingway anyway) knows his way around Paris. There are more such passages— "I got on an S bus and rode down to the Madeleine, standing on the back platform. From the Madeleine I walked along the Boulevard des Capucines to the Opéra, and up to my office." Or, "I went out onto the sidewalk and walked down toward the Boulevard St. Michel, passed the tables of the Rotonde, still crowded, looked across the street at the Dome, its tables running out to the edge of the pavement." Or, "The taxi went up the hill, passed the lighted square, then on into the dark, still climbing, then levelled out onto a dark street behind St. Etienne du Mont. . . ." And lest anyone suppose these data are coming (like Joyce's glimpses of Gibraltar) from a map and some picture postcards, we are given what is obviously first-hand sentiment:

> The Boulevard Raspail always made dull riding. It was like a certain stretch on the P.L.M. between Fontainebleau and Montereau that always made me feel bored and dead and dull until it was over. I suppose it is some association of ideas that makes those dead places in a journey. There are other streets in Paris as ugly as the Boulevard Raspail. It is a street I do not mind walking down at all. But I cannot stand to ride along it. Perhaps I had read something about it once. That was the way Robert Cohn was about all of Paris. I wondered where Cohn got that incapacity to enjoy Paris. Possibly from Mencken. Mencken hates Paris, I believe. So many young men get their likes and dislikes from Mencken.

"Remarks," Miss Stein said, "are not literature," and Ernest Hemingway was listening, but not always. To be knowing about young men and Mencken, to be knowing about the Boulevard Raspail, to be knowing also about a certain stretch of line between Fontainebleau and Montereau, and also about associations of ideas, such were temptations too gross to be resisted sometimes, and two excuses, the excuse that one more stroke was being added to Robert Cohn's character and the overriding excuse of needful specificity, allowed him to accommodate what tempted him without sleeping badly after his day's writing.

Of course he knew about fly-fishing as well, and bull-fighting, and the way of angling for marlin, and of shooting ducks, and about Valpolicella, which is not a *grand vin*, so that "bottling it and putting years on it only adds sediment," and his method of selective itemization permitted him to cascade these knowledges from hand to hand, often

by way of establishing the want of savvy evinced by characters we are to think less well of. If Fitzgerald's characters
are discriminated by what they do with their opportunities,
chiefly fiscal ones, Hemingway's are divided by their knowledge or ignorance of what the self-sufficient man ought to
know. This includes knowledge of what is and is not done,
an area of knowledge on which he displayed as much pains
as Henry James, though he was less troubled by fussy
distinctions.

Robert Cohn, for instance, is presented in the second
sentence of *The Sun Also Rises* as a man insufficiently
aware of pugilistic hierarchies:

> Robert Cohn was once middleweight boxing champion of
> Princeton. Do not think that I am very much impressed by that
> as a boxing title, but it meant a lot to Cohn.

Catching the interplay between two characters, the knowl-
edgeable narrator and the somewhat innocent Cohn, the
novel proceeds brilliantly, a sure sense of how things happen to the fall guy connecting sentence with sentence. For
the first time, Cohn is made to feel Jewish:

> He took it out in boxing, and he came out of Princeton
> with painful self-consciousness and the flattened nose, and was
> married by the first girl who was nice to him.

—a *New Yorker* short story ten years before that genre
existed; and note the precision of "was married by." Next
sentence:

> He was married five years, had three children, lost most
> of the fifty thousand dollars his father left him, the balance of
> the estate having gone to his mother, hardened into a rather
> unattractive mould under domestic unhappiness with a rich
> wife; and just when he had made up his mind to leave his wife
> she left him and went off with a miniature-painter.

—another *New Yorker* story.

> As he had been thinking for months about leaving his wife

and had not done it because it would be too cruel to deprive her of himself, her departure was a very healthful shock.

—another *New Yorker* story. The narrator's (and author's) knowingness is functional here, a sharp catty understanding of the things that happen to men who are not quite with it inflecting with motivation and with crisis sentences that can seem to the hurried reader as blank as earthworms.

The other brand of Hemingway knowingness is knowing *how*. When you know how to do a thing you do it gracefully, and until you have learned how to do a thing gracefully you should not be letting anyone see you do it. This is the code of the bullfighter, also of the writer, also of the dandy whose every gesture is a detail in that transient work of art, his public career.

The young William Butler Yeats once vexed his father by defining truth as "the dramatically appropriate utterance of the highest man." After utterance has lapsed dramatic appropriateness abides; and in a more reticent generation than Yeats's, Hemingway discerned truth in the fighting of bulls, and tragic eloquence in Pedro Romero's gestures.

Romero never made any contortions, always it was straight and pure and natural in line. The others twisted themselves like corkscrews, their elbows raised, and leaned against the flanks of the bull after his horns had passed, to give a faked look of danger. Afterward, all that was faked turned bad and gave an unpleasant feeling. Romero's bull-fighting gave real emotion, because he kept the absolute purity of line in his movements and always quietly and calmly let the horns pass him close each time.

The twisters like corkscrews are of course like rhetoricians, and Romero keeping purity of line is offering us the sight of what actually happens—"what the actual things were which produced the emotion that you experienced," as Hemingway later formulated his writer's canon on the second page of a book about the bull ring.

> *The rhetorician would deceive his neighbour,*

wrote Yeats,

> *The sentimentalist himself; while art*
> *Is but a vision of reality.*
> *What portion of the world can the artist have*
> *Who has awakened from the common dream*
> *But dissipation and despair?*

It would be simple to equip all Hemingway's stories with mottoes drawn from the poems of Yeats, and to parallel his theoretical pronouncements with passages from the Yeats *Essays* and the Yeats *Autobiography*, so completely, beneath his stoical, laconic disguise, is Hemingway committed to a view of life that belongs to the years in which Yeats's mind was formed, the late years of Walter Pater's nineteenth century. His model for the perfection of a style is the perfection of a life, which means the absolute mastery of the techniques appropriate to any moment of crisis. Thus Yeats in September 1909 tried to account for his impression that a certain stranger was vulgar, and observed that the man "moved from his head only."

> His arm and hand, let us say, moved in direct obedience to the head, had not the instinctive motion that comes from a feeling of weight, of the shape of an object to be touched or grasped. There were too many straight lines in gesture and in pose. The result was an impression of vulgar smartness, a defiance of what is profound and old and simple.

Francis Macomber in a similar way solicited instruction of how to shoot the lion—

> "If I get a shot, where should I hit him," Macomber asked, "to stop him?"
> "In the shoulders," Wilson said. "In the neck if you can make it. Shoot for bone. Break him down."
> "I hope I can place it properly," Macomber said.
> "You shoot very well," Wilson told him. "Take your time. Make sure of him. The first one in is the one that counts."
> "What range will it be?"

—asking the guide to program his arm and hand so that they will move in direct obedience to the head. The impression this talk leaves is less of vulgar smartness than of fear, but one can be sure that the guide (who very soon "looked at him quickly") detects a component of vulgarity. And sure enough, Francis Macomber, lacking as he does "the instinctive motion that comes from a feeling of weight, of the shape of an object to be touched or grasped"—the feel of the compressed act of shooting a lion—does not achieve the shot that counts, finds himself standing there "feeling sick at his stomach," and a little later, "the next thing he knew he was running."

He blew it, naturally. In competitive sports you blow it if you think. "I was going up to the plate," said a California ballplayer, 1970, "and thinking this elbow should be here and this one there and my wrist up here and my body positioned this way. I had so damn many things to think about that before I knew it the ball was by me." (And "Every time you think," said a coach, "you hurt the ball club.")

Eliot spoke of the "direct sensuous apprehension of thought," and Yeats of inexperienced actors who "show by the movement of their body that their idea of doing it is more vivid than the doing of it." If a woman's body, sinking into a chair, does not feel the size and shape of the chair before she reaches it, "she will never be able to act, just as she will never have grace of movement in ordinary life." One notes how close together are acting on the stage and the fact of grace in ordinary life, and notes also the "primitive" canons of Yeats's next sentence:

As I write I see through the cabin door [he was on shipboard] a woman feeding a child with a spoon. She thinks of nothing but the child and every movement is full of expression. It would be beautiful acting.

And a month later he wrote, "A good writer should be so simple that he has no faults, only sins."

Purpose inseparably fused with execution, no tinny ideas intervening, this ideal was widely voiced in the early twentieth century. D. H. Lawrence, excoriating "sex in the head," applied it to bodily intimacies. Wyndham Lewis, no lover of Lawrence, affirmed (1919) that the artist drew on impulses "older than the fish," and worked at the prompting of an immensely primitive will. Remy de Gourmont published (1903) in the wake of Fabre his *Physique de l'Amour: Essai sur l'Instinct Sexuel*, in which we learn what intricate things insects and animals may do without taking thought: in 1921 Ezra Pound translated it, with an enthusiastic postscript, meant to suggest how complexly creative an instinctive action might be. "Don't think," wrote Fitzgerald in requesting a judgment on a book. "Anybody can think." By 1950, in a good beginning to his feeblest novel, Ernest Hemingway could present a man shooting ducks so well that arm and hand move in communion with the descending birds, bypassing the ratiocinative faculty which only later appraises the quality of what instinct has accomplished (and you cannot explain your own poetry, Eliot said, because after it is written you come to it as a reader).

His head low, he swung the gun on a long slant, down, well and ahead of the second duck, then without looking at the result of his shot he raised the gun smoothly, up, up ahead and to the left of the other duck that was climbing to the left and as he pulled, saw it fold in flight and drop among the decoys in the broken ice. He looked to his right and saw the first duck a black patch on the same ice. He knew he had shot carefully on the first duck, far to the right of where the boat was, and on the second, high out and to the left, letting the duck climb far up and to the left to be sure the boat was out of any line of fire. It was a lovely double, shot exactly as he should have shot, with complete consideration and respect for the position of the boat, and he felt very good as he reloaded.

His care for the position of the boat had been subconscious. Francis Macomber would have discussed the boat with his guide, and then gone to pieces worrying about not hitting the boat, and then very likely perforated the boatman. (In 1973 a Maryland sportsman cracked four ribs executing an unlovely double; while he was taking aim on his second duck, the first dropped dead out of the sky on top of him.)

"It was a lovely double": a perfect moment: and in this spare lyrical prose it is recreated for as long and for as many times as there may be readers. Such perfect moments occur in flowing time, at the end of whose flow lies death, and if Hemingway is to be equipped with a sponsoring philosopher we shall not find one better qualified than Walter Pater, the aesthetician of appreciative intensities. "Each moment," Pater wrote, "some tint grows more perfect on land or sea"; all is flux, we are in flux with all, only so many pulse beats are granted us, and not to fix such perfections as we encounter is "to sleep before evening."

Who, in some such perfect moment, . . . has not felt the desire to perpetuate all that, just so, to suspend it in every particular circumstance, with the portrait of just that one spray of leaves lifted just so high against the sky, above the well, forever?

There is the key to innumerable Hemingway pages. His trees and streams are not "settings," they are transiences, never quite to recur, never at all to be re-experienced as now:

In the late summer of that year we lived in a house in a village that looked across the river and the plain to the mountains. In the bed of the river there were pebbles and boulders, dry and white in the sun, and the water was clear and swiftly moving and blue in the channels. Troops went by the house and down the road and the dust they raised powdered the leaves of the trees. The trunks of the trees too were dusty and the leaves fell early that year and we saw the troops marching along the road and the dust rising and leaves, stirred by the breeze, falling and the soldiers marching and afterward the road bare and white except for the leaves.

—So begins *A Farewell to Arms*; and it is the very first words—"in the late summer of that year"—that tell us how to receive what may look like, but is not, a "descriptive" passage. We shall never experience any of this again, runs the undercurrent below these four sentences: and the troops move as the water moves, not, however, to recur like the self-renewing water, but to fall with the dust and the leaves, passing from a neutral world as emptied of their passage as the bare white road on which lie the corpses of leaves. But we, who lived in a house in the village then, can perpetuate and fix the time we passed in that house, and the pebbles in the stream, and the stream's blue water, and the dust and the marching troops. Meanwhile the permanent things, even those, ache with transience; for though the pebbles and the sunlight will endure we shall not see them with the same eyes again. And the army disintegrates, and Frederic Henry is a different man forever, and Catherine Barkley dies of multiple hemorrhages. Of what else should anyone die, at the end of this book? Throughout it time has poured, an unstanchable flow; and what memory and prose have fixed is the brief being of what never again will be.

And with Walter Pater's melancholy goes Walter Pater's obligation, which was to maximize those special moments, and they could by definition only be moments when, though time's flow seems to cease, its pressure is most poignant. For inherent in the magic moment is its transience. Hence Ernest Hemingway's cult of ritual death, amid the Green Hills of Africa or in the bull ring. The bull-fighter need not wait for some tint to grow more perfect by land or sea. On a specified afternoon at a specified time he has an appointment with the moment of truth. These remarks, in connection with Hemingway, are not new. What has been less routinely noticed, since so much of his public rhetoric directed attention away from the pertinent terminology, is the wholly aesthetic basis of all his values: aesthetic, decadent, in the *fin de siècle* sense: the sense of the

forlorn aesthetes, Dowson and Symons, Pater and Oscar
Wilde. Wilde put himself in the way of prosecution to
fulfill his tragic ambitions. Since he had not the resources,
nor his age the dramatic idiom, for the writing of a tragedy,
why, he would live one. Living a destiny he cannot write,
or else flirts with in writing, a writer becomes as did Wilde
a public legend. Hemingway's suicide in the same way was
very nearly an aesthetic necessity. "Some burn damp faggots," Yeats wrote in lines to celebrate Major Gregory,

> . . . *others may consume*
> *The entire combustible world in one small room*
> *As though dried straw, and if we turn about*
> *The bare chimney is gone black out*
> *Because the work had finished in that flare.*
> *Soldier, scholar, horseman, he,*
> *As 'twere all life's epitome.*
> *What made us dream that he could comb grey hair?*

A romanticization, yes, of course, of course. That view of
life is one long romanticization. Hemingway's suicide, in
another terminology, came out of depression. One component of the depression, it seems plain, was the fear that he
could no longer write; and he owed it to his sense of fitness,
an aesthetic sense, not to burn damp faggots.

His sense of fitness went deeper than we may suppose.
Sensing the use of a role and a legend, he sensed also that
the artist's role had changed since the mind of a Yeats was
formed. In France, not in England, he received his intuition
of such matters with Cocteau's and Apollinaire's especial
torque: *it was necessary to pose as an impostor.*

Yeats had played the Poet. Later James Joyce, by a
delicate redistribution of psychic emphases, had contrived
to play the Indigent Man of Letters. (Yes, he was frequently indigent; yes, he was a man of letters; the meaning
of "contrived to play" is that he kept these facts somewhat

emphatically in view. And sometimes he utilized patent-leather shoes to play the man of letters as dandy.) T. S. Eliot in England played numerous roles, among them The American; on Faber & Faber stationery of the 1930's the words "U.S.A. Origin" appear bracketed after his name in the list of directors. Eliot's most interesting role was perhaps The Englishman, subspecies London Clubman. He played it not in America but in England, and in such a way as never to conceal the fact that he was playing. For no credit could attach to *being* a London clubman; one had only to be born to that life. The credit attached to mastery of the role, credit to be derived only if he made it clear, by small overemphases, that it *was* a role. One day, surpassing himself, he greeted a fellow member of the Garrick Club in accents of theatrical resignation: "I am not pretending that I am suffering from rheumatism. . . . [This alluded to the stick upon which he was leaning.] I no longer pretend that I am learned. . . . I no longer pretend I am pretending."

The role fixes the writer's location, detached from his material. Located in the role, drawing from its coordinate system his up and down, his left and right, he can then write "sincerely." Eliot, we must not forget, was an American, manipulating the American virtue of candor. If we grant that he was what his role of the moment made him, then speaking from the center of the role he was perfectly candid.

> *And I pray that I may forget*
> *These matters that with myself I too much discuss*
> *Too much explain*
> *Because I do not hope to turn again*
> *Let these words answer*
> *For what is done, not to be done again . . .*

He is being candid about the miserable fate of his marriage to Vivien Haigh-Wood. The candor is made tolerable, poetically tolerable as well as psychically, by the role he plays in *Ash-Wednesday*: the role of a minor poet apprenticing himself to Dante.

Hemingway, American likewise, learned one role early, that of Special Correspondent, professionally detached from public horrors which he owed it to his readers to write down. "So the mob swarmed down and tried to push the policeman loose into the current. It meant drowning for the policeman to let go—and he hung on. Then the mob chopped his fingers loose from the stone with the hatchet with which they had been attacking the statue." This role, in the inter-chapters of *In Our Time*, established a center from which to write of private horrors as well, and we can tell from the swept and tidied prose of those stories how readily it could blend into another role, that of the martyr to literature, starving while he sought to write One True Sentence. It was in this capacity that he visited Gertrude Stein, who later remembered that "Even when he was poor the holes in his clothes were overdone."

"One true sentence" sounds like a parody. It will lose the sound of parody if an exact context is devised for it, which means an exact role. We have it in the context Ernest Hemingway devised for it late in the 1950's, when he wrote in a tone of fond astringency the book he said might be regarded as fiction, about a young man named Hemingway writing in Paris:

> But sometimes when I was starting a new story and I could not get it going, I would sit in front of the fire and squeeze the peel of the little oranges into the edge of the flame and watch the sputter of blue that they made. I would stand and look out over the roofs of Paris and think, "Do not worry. You have always written before and you will write now. All you have to do is write one true sentence. Write the truest sentence that you know." So finally I would write one true sentence, and then go on from there. It was easy then because there was always one true sentence that I knew or had seen or had heard someone say.

There "one true sentence" isn't a Mauberley's fantasy, but part of a ritual of self-hypnosis, one of the innumerable rituals, from sharpening twenty pencils to pitching cards into a hat, that writers have devised to get themselves started. The sentence, moreover, is not something he must laboriously construct, like Flaubert, but something already there, to be recalled and written down. It will be worth the considerable discipline of recalling it, recognizing it and not deforming it, because once written down in his firm clear handwriting it will work like the scrap of real wall-paper in a cubist *collage*: the scrap of authenticity that will generate the story. That was Hemingway's role, then, the recorder of authenticities. It grew out of his role as a journalist, protecting him, now that he was writing *stories*, from the *littérateur's* temptations. And it grew into a further role, the experiencer of authenticities to be recorded. "It was easy then," he recalled of the early 1920's, "because there was always one true sentence that I knew. . . ." It was less easy when he had used them up. Hence, a few years later, the "primitive" quest after ultimates, the making of love, the giving of death, on which he founded a public persona that could behave as if it had no talent except for boozing and bragging.

Hence the paradox that the biography of Hemingway does not seem to be the biography of the writer but of some-body else, somebody of whom we must postulate that mys-teriously, at intervals, he wrote. If we fix our attention on that persona, then it is the writer who seems to be the impostor. What is the lion-killer doing at a writing-desk? Even standing up at it? Or leafing through the extracts from Donne's sermons in *The Oxford Book of English Prose* in quest of a title for his Spanish novel? Or priding himself on forty-three consecutive chapters "with every word de-pending on every other word"? We are less surprised to know that when he finished the Spanish book he then helped kill 400 jackrabbits, and was soon dictating the terms on which the book was to be sold to the movies. Later he told some professors in Honolulu that it had been for years his habit to read Donne, on Sundays.

Donne in archaic spelling on the flyleaf of *For Whom the Bell Tolls*—"No man is an *Iland*, intire of it selfe"—comports with a sham-archaic peasant philosophizing, somewhat protected by the postulation of another language:

... I would like to have it so that I could tie a handkerchief to that bush back there and come in the daylight and take the eggs and put them under a hen and be able to see the chicks of the partridge in my own courtyard. I would like such small and regular things.

But you have no house and no courtyard to your no-house, he thought. You have no family but a brother who goes to battle tomorrow and you own nothing but the wind and the sun and an empty belly. The wind is small, he thought, and there is no sun. You have four grenades in your pocket but they are only good to throw away. You have a carbine on your back but it is only good to give away bullets. You have a message to give away. And you're full of crap that you can give to the earth, he grinned in the dark. You can anoint it also with urine. Everything you have is to give. Thou art a phenomenon of philosophy and an unfortunate man, he told himself and grinned again.

This is Hemingway talking to us, quite aware that he could not talk in this way save at a double remove: (1) the stylizer of (2) a Spanish guerrilla's reflections.

"Full of crap" is American demotic. "I would like such small and regular things" is a philosophic paraphrase of Homer, whose warrior wished only to see the smoke go up again from his father's home, and after that to die. "Thou art a phenomenon of philosophy" is Hemingway's baroque-Falstaffian way of apologizing, with an embarrassed grin, for putting on display such a show of profundity. And the whole passage uses history to deny history: there is only, when you come down to it, dung and death, and John Donne himself is quaint. When the bridge blows up, the orgasmic moment toward which 445 pages have strained, a Neolithic unreflectiveness is synthesized to string out Robert Jordan's sensations in an array that no Oak Park schoolteacher would call a sentence:

> . . . and he dug his heels in and leaned back hard onto the tension of the wire with a turn of it around his wrist and the noise of the truck was coming behind and ahead there was the road with the dead sentry and the long bridge and the stretch of road below, still clear and then there was a cracking roar and the middle of the bridge rose up in the air like a wave breaking and he felt the blast from the explosion roll back against him as he dove on his face in the pebbly gully with his hands holding tight over his head.

The nearest thing that is being exploded here, as the string of and's may alert us, is an Old Testament cadence; as for instance,

> *And* Samson took hold of the two middle pillars upon which the house stood, *and* on which it was borne up, of the one with his right hand, *and* of the other with his left. *And* Samson said, Let me die with the Philistines. *And* he bowed himself with all his might, *and* the house fell upon the lords, *and* upon all the people that were therein.

This is remote, ceremonious (its English is nearly contemporary with Donne's). Immediacy deletes its ritual pauses, as of the mind appraising, articulating; immediacy liquefies reflection into pure serial sensation; yet immediacy's unemphatic blankness to the reading eye becomes cadence once more to the listening ear, a detectable Biblical cadence, at once affirmed and denied.

So style cancels "style." Leaking from the prose into the events the prose celebrates, style also cancels events and cancels time, asserting that the things men do are few things only, slight in variety, meager in result (what is one blown bridge, one dead bull?), satisfying only when they are done accurately and well, which means done with style. So history vanishes and history's wisdom; history has too little substance to occupy the mind: only a few violences. "As a

poet," Gary Snyder has written (1961), "I hold the most
archaic values on earth. They go back to the Neolithic: the
fertility of the soil, the magic of animals, the power-vision in
solitude, the terrifying initiation and rebirth, the love and
ecstasy of the dance, the common work of the tribe. A gas
turbine or an electric motor is a finely-crafted flint knife in
the hand. It is useful and full of wonder, but it is not our
whole life." This assertion rhymes with a dismissal of the
content of history, which requires only thirty words: "America five hundred years ago was clouds of birds, miles of
bison, endless forests and grass and clear water. Today it is
the tired ground of the world's dominant culture." So much
for Thomas Jefferson and Tom Paine; so much for the
Adamses and Emerson and Agassiz; so much for you, Henry
James. And sing, Muse, if you have tongue, what would
have been the judgment of Henry James on a novelist for
whom thirty centuries of civilization, all the long effort
since Homer and Thucydides, has for its quintessence only
a moment of which this is the dialogue:

"Maria."
"Yes."
"Maria."
"Yes."
"Maria."
"Oh, yes. Please."
"Art thou not cold?"
"Oh, no. Pull the robe over thy shoulders."
"Maria."
"I cannot speak."
"Oh, Maria. Maria. Maria."

and for whom a good life, remembered amid privations, is a
litany of sensations, for instance smells:

That must be the odor of nostalgia, the smell of the smoke
from the piles of raked leaves burning in the streets in the
fall in Missoula. Which would you rather smell? Sweet grass
the Indians used in their baskets? Smoked leather? The odor

of the ground in the spring after rain? The smell of the sea as you walk through the gorse on a headland in Galicia? Or the wind from the land as you come in toward Cuba in the dark? That was the odor of the cactus flowers, mimosa and the sea-grape shrubs. . . .

"Live all you can," a middle-aged James character had exhorted a young one: "Live all you can; it's a mistake not to. . . . Do what you like so long as you don't make *my* mistake. For it was a mistake. Live!" But James meant more by "Live!", one cannot help thinking, than the knack of so arranging one's priorities that one would one day have a girl and the memory of smells.

Hemingway had a sharp eye, once, for Sherwood Anderson's mannerisms, and the value they placed on primitive uncomplication. That Anderson wrote simple, clean prose is a critics' commonplace; that his prose had but a few uses, readily inventoried, is a point less often made. It is a prose in which to tell of lonely people doing things they have no way of thinking about, supposing as they do, off there in the provinces, that their impulses and their troubles are unique. The stories are meant to appeal to more knowing people than the people they are about, which explains the presence of some of them in *The Little Review* ("the magazine that is read by those who write the others") and explains also why for some years Anderson's future was expensively backed by Horace Liveright, the sophistication specialist. Like most exploitable sophistication, Anderson's is pretty facile. A clergyman in *Winesburg, Ohio* wrestles with what he can only call "the flesh," represented by a woman glimpsed through her window next door from his window in the church tower. Later when he sees her kneeling naked, praying, he smashes a stained-glass pane with a fist into which has come what he calls "the strength of God." The reader is meant to recognize sexual energy. Or a widower's

life is dominated by daughters, a "good" daughter and a
"bad" one. When he thrashes the bad one, and later in the
night hears both girls softly laughing, he lies bewildered,
sleepless. A reader who has heard of Freud will feel no
bewilderment.

Hemingway's readers, on the contrary, have often been
bewildered, because though he too, like Anderson, developed the knack of telling simultaneously an overt story
and a hidden one, the hidden Hemingway story is not
reducible to notions out of a handbook. For years one of
his most remarkable accomplishments, "Big Two-Hearted
River," was accepted as a fine narrative about fishing; not
until 1944 was it described (by Malcolm Cowley) as an
account of ritualized escape "from a nightmare or from
realities that have become a nightmare."

A terrible panic [Philip Young wrote a few years later]
is just barely under control, and the style—this is the "Hemingway style" at its most extreme—is the perfect expression of
the content of the story.

Nick's mechanical movements—of cooking, casting, bait-
ing his hook and the rest—are the mindless movements of, say,
a woman who all alone busies herself with a thorough house-
cleaning on the morning after the sudden death of her husband,
or the movements of the hands of a badly shell-shocked veteran,
who, while he can control himself, is performing simple jobs
over and over in a factory: this, and then that. . . . This is the
whole "point" of an otherwise pointless story. . . .

—the last story, moreover, of the book called *In Our Time*
("Give us peace in our time, O Lord") where so many
traumatic assaults are undergone by protagonist and by
reader. If that book was so little understood for so long, one
may ask why it was so respected. The clean writing, obviously, seemed (and is) admirable, the refreshing closeness
of the prose to physical experience. In much the same way,
the nightingale's song is enjoyed by naïve ears that do not
know what the nightingale is saying:

> *The change of Philomel, by the barbarous king*
> *So rudely forced.*

The barbarous king, Tereus, raped her and cut out her tongue; Eliot, whose *Waste Land* also contains sweet singing that does not disclose what horrors it sings about, enforced his theme by having her sing "Tereu."

As Eliot's miserable first marriage lies behind *The Waste Land*, impelling the woman who on one occasion says,

> *"My nerves are bad to-night. Yes, bad. Stay with me.*
> *"Speak to me. Why do you never speak. Speak. . . ."*

and on another, still more unnervingly,

> *"You gave me hyacinths first a year ago;*
> *"They called me the hyacinth girl."*

so many traumata Hemingway had experienced, and notably the shrapnel wound near Fossalta, July 8, 1918, when "his legs felt as if he were wearing rubber boots filled with warm water," are implicit in the stories of *In Our Time*: a poem, therefore, and a book of stories each distinguished by a lyric economy never eloquent about its real causes. Each of them, the book and the poem, is a succession of apparently unrelated fragments. Each of them appears to gather up and symbolize, comprehensively, the times. Each is autobiographical at bottom, but so indirectly, especially the poem, that the detailed pertinence of the author's life is apt to surprise us when we finally learn about it. And both writers have subscribed, in different words, to the doctrine of the Objective Correlative.

Which turns out, therefore, to be a somewhat misleading doctrine. Putting down "what the actual things were which produced the emotion that you experienced" suggests a rhetoric of candor; and while Eliot and Hemingway seem to be doing that, their real triumph lies in a rhetoric of evasion. Hemingway at his best—and his best is in his stories, the device being almost impossible to sustain at novel length—is never really writing about what he seems to be. He achieves this indirection in various ways. "Big Two-Hearted River" resembles the Parable of the Sower in offering so simple a narrative content that we are meant to realize there is more to it than there seems to be. The dialogue in "Hills Like White Elephants" studs dry evasiveness with so many silences that we soon commence to fill in the unspoken bits, and realize that the man and the woman are deliberately not mentioning the abortion that obsesses them both. They are distracted by distraction, but not (as in Eliot's phrase) from distraction: from horror. In "A Clean Well-Lighted Place," as in the trout stream Nick Adams fished, we have a focus of ritual distraction from engulfments that will not submit to being ritualized: a symbol, then, of the use to which the mind, or the world, puts taxonomies when the fear of non-being besets it.

And one remarkable story, "After the Storm," aligns itself with a tradition of symbolism stemming from Pater's discovery that a woman's portrait—the *Mona Lisa*—was a symbol of all that men had come to desire, and assesses the meaning of the submarine beings—Rhine-maidens, Lorelei, sea-maids in Prufrock's "chambers of the sea"—that have lured the Western imagination for nearly two centuries. Hemingway's water is perfectly real: the narrator's lungs nearly burst with the effort to stay under it, and his nose bleeds from the effort to overcome its buoyancy. The woman is real too, and drowned; he glimpses her face in its frame of floating hair, gazing blindly up through the porthole of a sunken liner, "as big as the whole world," that lies on its side at a depth just below his diving range. It is her jewels that lure him; he bangs on the porthole glass with his wrench, but cannot break it, and loses the wrench and watches it slide down the curved side of the ship and into darkness. The story is a triumph of factual writing, word lying close to physical sensation in a world where the phy-

sical is whelmingly pertinent because the very limitations
of life in the body—buoyancy, the need to breathe, cold,
fatigue—are what frustrate a quest so bizarre it passes without effort from fact to symbol. In this strange, triumphantly
realized story there is for once no indirection, the "meaning"
lying not to one side of the narrative but directly before us,
in the depths of the narrative. Though Hemingway's scav-
enger is the kind of primitive, uncomplicated being that
clear prose such as Anderson's and Hemingway's own had
been evolved to deal with, "After the Storm" marks Hemingway's furthest reach past the sociological simplicities of
Anderson.

Simple prose for simple matters—not Jamesian matters, but
for instance a father's rage at his slatternly daughter—is in
theory a decorous meeting of simplicities, in practice a
writer's minefield. Thus Anderson's "Daughters" ends with
a silly little paragraph:

> The sound of the whispering continued. Girls were some-
> thing you couldn't understand. There was something . . . it was
> hidden from you. How strange it was!

—not uncharacteristic, for when he tried to articulate his
characters' incomprehensions, Anderson was often betrayed
into silliness. In *Dark Laughter*, the target of Hemingway's
celebrated parody, the betrayal is almost continuous. A paragraph of banal perhapses ends by asserting that "A mind
like Bruce's sought explanations for everything." An account of dark song from the world of dark laughter—
"Sounds caught and held in black throats. Notes split into
quarter-notes. The word, as meaning, of no importance.
Perhaps words were always unimportant"—culminates in
what is meant for a vision of wholeness:

> Brown bodies trotting, black bodies trotting. The bodies
> of all the men running up and down the landing-stage were one

body. One could not be distinguished from another. They were lost in each other.

Could the bodies of people be so lost in each other? . . .

This in turn, a page later, stands for "the strangeness and wonder of things," lost to grown white men. "Perhaps white men's getting on so fast in life, having newspapers, advertising, great cities, smart clever minds, ruling the world, had cost them more than they had gained. They hadn't gained much." Horace Liveright's advertising reached the smart, clever minds whose approval confers bestsellerdom, and 22,297 copies of *Dark Laughter* had been sold within three months. It was Sherwood Anderson's one commercial success.

In *The Torrents of Spring*, which Allen Tate was to call the most economically realized humor of disproportion he had read in American prose, Hemingway kidded its mannerisms without mercy. (" 'See you all later,' he said. He went out into the night. It seemed the only thing to do. He did it.") Nevertheless, in *A Farewell to Arms* and *For Whom the Bell Tolls* we encounter a schematism similar to Anderson's, only written in less vulnerable prose. Like Anderson's Negroes, Hemingway's philosophical Spanish peasants epitomize the unillusioned life, and his Robert Jordan, a language professor whom guerrilla warfare has brought into a condition of cherishing the memory of smells and the palpability of Maria as ultimates by which to test mere ideas, is like some Anderson protagonist restored to the wholeness of boyhood. In *Dark Laughter* the grown Bruce wonders if this is possible. "The strangeness and the wonder of things—in nature—he had known as a boy and that he had somehow later lost—the sense lost living in a city and being married to Bernice—could he get it back again?" Yes he could, *For Whom the Bell Tolls* would seem to answer; what Robert Jordan had lost presiding over classrooms he got back in Spain, in a sleeping-bag, under the shadow of death. It was to establish such a possibility that Hemingway ran the risks inherent in monosyllabic dialogue ("Maria." "Yes." "Maria." "Yes." "Maria."). Where Anderson rhapsodizes, Hemingway is stoical on principle, for it inheres in his dream of recovered wholeness that no analytic words may penetrate it.

The quest of the one true sentence leads to wordlessness; that is the irony of Hemingway's aesthetic. And if, to get a novel written, wordlessness must be filled with words, they will verge on the parodic. Joyce began *Ulysses* in naturalism and ended it in parody, understanding more profoundly than any of his followers that naturalism cannot end anywhere else, and a law like the hidden law that governs the unfolding of styles in *Ulysses* brought Hemingway to self-parody at last, as though, not understanding the history disclosed by Joyce, he was condemned to repeat it. Hence the debacle of *Across the River and Into the Trees*, which Hemingway thought unbearable in its emotion, but which a *New Yorker* wit had no trouble pillorying as twenty-five years previously *The Torrents of Spring* had pilloried *Dark Laughter*.

The quest of the one true sentence leads to wordlessness. In one of Hemingway's most famous passages, Lieutenant Frederic Henry concluded that in a politicians' war his life and countless lives were imperiled by nothing more than a false semantics:

> I was always embarrassed by the words sacred, glorious, and sacrifice and the expression in vain. We had heard them, sometimes standing in the rain almost out of earshot, so that only the shouted words came through . . . and I had seen nothing sacred, and the things that were glorious had no glory and the sacrifices were like the stockyards at Chicago if nothing was done with the meat except to bury it. . . . Abstract words such as glory, honor, courage, or hallow were obscene. . . .

These words alone, these fictions, he concludes, are driving him to certain death, so he jumps into a river and deserts, saved, as it were, by a stylistic insight such as discriminates Ernest Hemingway's prose from Woodrow Wilson's.

To write off the big empty words is to return to the small full words, small because Saxon and rooted, full because intimate with physical sensation, the ground, the knowable. But the small full words have dangers of their own; they tend to contract and grow fewer, and approximate to the grunt. In the early 1960's the hidden guru of the magazine called *Playboy* was spinning off installments of an interminable "philosophy," later distributed in pamphlet form to a mailing list that included select academics thought of as in need of evangelization, or perhaps as ripe for conversion. Like most jokes for the sophisticated, it concealed a different point; for in being polysyllabic the guru was avoiding, by sure instinct, the perils of being laconic. Had he been laconic, *Playboy* would have been driven toward a one-word philosophy, such being the dynamic of small words. One feels sure what the word would be, a word Hemingway without evident deprivation did without, a word that attaches to many "perfect moments" but does little to help recapture them. That was his drive, he thought, to recapture perfect moments: to put down "what the actual things were which produced the emotion that you experienced." But that drive was menaced, perfect moments were encroached on, by a different small word, which he preferred in its Spanish form, *nada*. We see it surrounding "A Clean Well-Lighted Place," and the light holding it at bay.

Fighting off *nada* was his conscious drive, but only a small part of his achievement. His achievement, seldom vouchsafed to the novels but often to the stories, consisted in setting down, so sparely that we can see past them, the words for the action that concealed the real action: Nick Adams fishing, not thinking, very deliberately not thinking of the shadows, or the protagonist of "After the Storm" withheld by the very limits of the body from satisfying his almost bodily greed for the rings on the fingers of the submarine Venus, her dead face afloat amid its floating hair beneath that impregnable glass between what is quick and what is still.

VI⁄Classroom Accuracies

Ezra Pound, poet, and T. S. Eliot, poet, emerged from what would now be called Comparative Literature classrooms, the one at Penn and Hamilton, the other at Harvard. Consequently they got started quickly. Work each of them had done by the end of 1909 still figures in their winnowed collections: Pound's "La Fraisne" and "Cino," for instance, Eliot's "Conversation Galante." Dr. William Carlos Williams, by contrast, though in 1909 he actually published a book of twenty-six poems, entitled *Poems*, was never to reprint a single one of them, and no wonder:

> *I've fond anticipation of a day*
> *O'erfilled with pure diversion presently,*
> *For I must read a lady poesie*
> *The while we glide by many a leafy bay . . .*

The "lady" was H.D., Ezra Pound's old girl friend, for whom he had written "The Tree" that still opens *Personae*. The book—such was Williams' competitiveness—may have been in part a response to Pound's *A Lume Spento* of the previous year: also privately printed, though in Venice, not Rutherford. Emulation chalked up no further scores. There is not a line in *Poems* worth keeping. This false start, and his belated real start, may reflect the fact that Williams was never in a college literature classroom, not until, decades later, he lectured in them.

Not that classrooms produce poets, or have ever produced them; but classrooms do generate structures in the mind. They can be, one frequenter has testified, "magical" places. A blackboard by the end of the hour, scrawled with recondite graffiti, is fertile in enigmatic juxtapositions; a lecturer who can make things clear may inadvertently demonstrate how also to make them comic; a curriculum is a grand time-bound surrealism. To ask what Shakespeare would have made of a course on Jacobean Drama is to glimpse the nearly Cubist perspectives a course can impose on what, otherwise regarded, is "experience." In particular a whole literature, the sum of many writers' *seriatim* acts, can become a bounded mental construction, with single remembered lines and phrases and idioms for its coordinate points. The same can happen to a whole language. It is only in classrooms that one thinks of whole languages. Out in the world where men buy shirts and order meals, French phrases or German phrases are alternate ways of saying what you can also say in English. In the classroom such options are minimal; the French 1 student "says it in English" to demonstrate, sometimes, his understanding of French, but it's understood that his mind for the duration belongs in French, is understood to dwell in "French," a mental place and not the same as "France." And he thinks much about the big and little words. Lieutenant Henry's creator, though not a college man, frequented colleges, and touched on fashionable classroom themes of the 1920's when he had his lieutenant dwell skeptically on glory (*la gloire*) and honor (*l'honneur*).

Speculations on language, though not the effort of mastering languages, have a special appeal for Americans, inhabiting as they do the world's first classroom civilization. (From Grimm to Furnivall, the great linguistic empiricists were European; from Whorf to Chomsky, the great theorists have been American.) Being the first country since the rise of the nation-states to have undertaken to operate without a capital, America has evolved the university network, formally powerless but transcending regions and boundaries, and shaping the American sensibility more decisively than any other fact of public life.

"Without a capital" means without any one place to which power flows and from which judgment emanates. Washington is a "capital" of sorts, being where the government is kept, but one does not go there save as the government enters one's motivations. It is not because it is where you find the French government that Paris has been sought out for centuries. New York is a place sought out, but because it's where many sorts of jobs are: a *financial* capital, not otherwise taken seriously. Of course, since visibility feeds on money, New York is the place of maximum visibility, and if your activities require that you be highly visible, then like Andy Warhol you may find New York indispensable. Warhol has made art out of sheer publicity, as Michelangelo made it out of marble, the substance of his gestures so perfectly weightless that we have no need to see the actual autographed soup tins, and New York is the place for that.

Otherwise, no capitals, except in the metaphorical sense in which Hollywood is called the movie capital and Detroit the motor capital (and little of the appropriate activity, for that matter, goes on any longer in either of those places). The American intuition has been to disperse, not to concentrate: to put the New York state legislature not in New York but in a place called Albany of which foreigners have no need to hear; to issue *Poetry*, the American Muse's

Reuters, decade after decade from Chicago, the "Hog Butcher for the World" as a Muse once had it; to scatter poets and novelists from Milledgeville, Ga., to Brooklyn, N.Y., and Albuquerque, N.M., with no reason whatever why they should frequent a common salon. A Gothic imagination sufficient to propel a French career of esteem haunted the skull of Ralph Eugene Meatyard (1925–1972), a photographer in Lexington, Kentucky. There was no reason he should leave there. And a South Carolinian come to settle in Lexington (by way of Harvard and Haverford) had no way of knowing about Meatyard's proximity until word came, unofficially, round the university circuit, from Highlands, N.C. This is a normative anecdote.

Intelligence travels round the network, not as well as it might, but travels. More pertinently, half the youth of America now go on to what is called "higher education." Two men who have sometime, somewhere, been to college have always something to talk about if they are thrown together at a strange airport. Similarly an Alabaman and a Vermonter who have both been to college will have more in common than will two North Dakotans one of whom has and one of whom has not. The "subject" of college, we may even say, is college.

All this is new in the world: post-World War II, in fact. Within living memory, even in America, college meant sports chiefly. Typical of a still earlier order of things, the young Samuel Johnson when he came out of Litchfield headed at once for London. It was inconceivable that his destiny, even as a lexicographer, should be Oxford. He did spend time at Oxford, time largely wasted. Oxford was dead. But look for a Nobel laureate in America today, and you are nearly sure to find him on some university faculty; likewise many poets and some novelists; likewise designers, architects, economists. The campus is even the alternative occupation of former cabinet secretaries, former vice-presidents. Such facts affect American letters profoundly. Even

Faulkner in his last years, Faulkner who proudly had no truck with intellectualisms, was to be found most likely at a university address, Virginia at one time, West Point at another.

Faulkner is also studied in college classrooms: was studied in them in his lifetime. So is any writer you are likely to name. Seminar attention is what is brought to bear on work increasingly disregardful of what "the public" will bring to it, because the active public is on campus, and capable, as the Tolkien phenomenon showed in the late 1960's, of making reputations for books whose trade sales have been sluggish. Increasingly there are two orders of literary reputation: that charted by bestsellerdom, for which the old reviewing and bookselling system suffices, and that registered in campus bookstores, chiefly paperback and often catered to by very small houses. The latter has proved the perennial despair of publishers who have tried to organize reliable access to it. Its sanctions have largely replaced the sterile *succès d'estime* Horace Liveright was courting when he manufactured 1,000 copies of the 64-page *Waste Land* (salmon dust-wrapper printed in black; outer glassine wrapper). Poets, consequently, have in America today a larger head-count of readers than any poets in the previous history of the world, anomalies like Tennyson excepted. For one Englishman who in 1671 could have identified Andrew Marvell (known from manuscript copies, privately circulated), a thousand young Americans can identify Robert Creeley: this thanks to the seminar and the paperback. That is how verse exists in the 1970's; it thrusts itself straight into the classroom. There are worse places for a phoenix to perform its fiery rite.

Early in the 1940's, just before the campus network began to assert itself, a crisis is identifiable, compounded of the war and the aftermath of the Depression. Every book of

Faulkner's was out of print, and, in a different realm, every book of Marianne Moore's. Only the devotion of James Laughlin explained the availability—against slow sales—of William Carlos Williams' *Complete Collected Poems*, published in 1938, and 506 copies bound in that year. Name-droppers (and review-page editors) were still unaware of Williams, and the post-war *Paterson* took them by surprise: "a New Jersey pediatrician," explained *Time*, "who versifies between cases." In such milieux Pound, if not excoriated, was forgotten. There were campus literati who read all these writers, but without thought of putting them on curricula. Even on campus *The Great Gatsby* was long forgotten, and its author dead after four years' hacking in Hollywood, his real-life equivalent of Dick Diver's upstate New York. Hemingway, unsurprisingly, rode the crest of the war; he was understood to be the time's *action* specialist. Alfred Knopf, also unsurprisingly, served tacit notice that Borzoi culture would continue, and published Stevens' *Parts of a World* in 1942. Sales were tepid. And Harcourt, Brace had Eliot in print.

So Eliot and Wallace Stevens existed, and Hemingway, their hairy opposite, existed. That was how the bookstore map of serious letters looked, though Hemingway's place on the map was problematical and really serious people preferred Kafka to any of them. It is not surprising at all that yet one more effort from the thirties had vanished entirely from sight, as if it had never been (and commercially speaking it hadn't): the work of the Objectivists, whose sometime allies Stevens and Williams had been.

Like all such groups—the Imagists, for instance—the Objectivist group had fluctuating boundaries. The usual list includes, in alphabetical order, George Oppen (b. 1908; University of Oregon; sometime publisher, tool-and-die maker, cabinetmaker, mechanic); Carl Rakosi (b. 1903; attendance at four campuses, degrees in English, psychology and social work, a psychotherapist); Charles Reznikoff (b.

1894; studies at Missouri and N.Y.U.; a lawyer); and Louis
Zukofsky (b. 1904; M.A. Columbia, 1924; college teacher
at Wisconsin, Colgate, and Brooklyn Polytechnic, from
which he was to retire in 1966 as Associate Professor of
English). They had college-formed minds, and were also
part of the large world, the exactions of which led Oppen
and Rakosi to give up poetry altogether for decades. They
were unsustained by the present-day campus network, which
about 1931 hadn't begun to exist. And since the publishing
network ignored them likewise (they were austere writers,
and a depression was in progress) they attained minimal
visibility: rather less, even, than Williams had before the
Complete Collected Poems equipped him with, at least, a
doughty book (317 pages, in "legal Buckram").

They were a "group," more or less, for a short time
only: long enough for the "Objectivist" number of *Poetry*
(February 1931) and *An "Objectivists" Anthology* (1932)
to bewilder the literate. Chiefly, they did their own publishing. Oppen, who had money in 1929, founded a little firm
in Toulon, France, to issue some useful items of out-of-print
Pound. It was called "TO Publishers," he later forgot why.
Zukofsky tells why, in remembering to have named it: "*To*
—as we might say, a health to—*To*." (The interest in preg-
nant little words is characteristic.) TO also issued *An
"Objectivists" Anthology*. Back in New York it became The
Objectivist Press, "an organization of writers who are publishing their own work and that of other writers whose work
they think ought to be read." The Objectivist Press ("Ad-
visory Board: Ezra Pound, William Carlos Williams, Louis
Zukofsky, *Sec'y*") issued Williams' *Collected Poems 1921–
1931*, a selection made by Zukofsky; and Oppen's *Discrete
Series*; and a little more; and faded. Oppen and Rakosi
stopped writing for years, Zukofsky worked away in total
obscurity at the long poem, "*A*," he'd begun in 1928; Reznikoff was prolific but uncelebrated. Upon being rediscovered
in the mid-1960's, they were all immediately asked, over and

over, by resurrection men who had done some homework, what "Objectivism" might have been and whether they still believed in it.

There was, the precise Zukofsky insists, never any such thing as "objectivism": no -ism, only -ists. "You must have a movement," Harriet Monroe had said, after commissioning him, at Pound's prodding, to edit the February 1931 *Poetry*. No, he said, some of us are writing to say things simply so that they will affect us as new again. "Well, give it a name."

As Visiting Editor he supplied an essay—"Sincerity and Objectification"—which (together with the poems) caused a Long Island subscriber to mail back his copy first class "with a letter demanding the price of it"; which has not won the total approval of any of the other Objectivists; which has been adverted to as a transcension of human understanding; and which nevertheless is worth elucidating. It was a serious effort, we may say, to go on from Hemingway's notion of the "one true sentence," itself a derivation of Imagism, and it confronts by implication Frederic Henry's *topos* of the big and the little words. If our sensibilities are no longer post-Imagist though we do not know why, a hidden reason may be Zukofsky's example, via other poets.

"Sincerity," the essay says, then "Objectification."

Sincerity is a beginning, to go on from. The True Sentence, Zukofsky helps us say, exemplifies Sincerity. In addition to lock-stitching a sequence of words to a perception, it affirms (a little conspicuously?) its composer's care, dedication and scrupulousness. Thus the beautiful, famous sentence, "In the fall the war was always there, but we did not go to it any more," is very nearly *unnaturally* beautiful, so contrived seems its elegiac balance. Though the words are common, no one ever spoke them in that combination. Yet it bespeaks care: sincerity. Zukofsky's instance of Sincerity was a one-line poem by Charles Reznikoff:

APHRODITE URANIA

The ceaseless weaving of the uneven water.

Each word, he noted, possesses "remarkable energy as an image of water as action." That is the first step toward sincerity: care for the single words. And "the title carries connotative and associative meaning in itself, and in relation to the line." Aphrodite is a water-born ceaselessness, and if we could see her in the intentness of our looking at water, it would be like the experience of thinking of that line, not one syllable of which fails to be woven with several others. "The mind is attracted to the veracity of the particular craft." Quite: the mind admires the accomplishment. A few more such lines, and the verse would be admiring its own accomplishment likewise. (All that mars *The Old Man and the Sea* is its admiration for itself, seemingly inseparable from fine finish.)

"Objectification," on the other hand, "is rare." "Properly no verse should be called a poem if it does not convey the totality of perfect rest"; for it is self-sufficient adequacy that the Objectivist prizes, not the glaze of accomplishment. Reznikoff again, cited by Zukofsky:

> How shall we mourn you who are killed and wasted,
> Sure that you would not die with your work unended—
> As if the iron scythe in the grass stops for a flower.

"Objectification in this poem is attained in the balance of the first two lines; the third line adds the grace of ornament in a simile, as might the design painted around a simple bowl." We look at the interaction of the lines, not at their rapport with their subject. We need not think of the subject. It is irrelevant, Zukofsky notes, to know that this was conceived as an epitaph for Gaudier-Brzeska. It is irrelevant likewise for us to observe that the first two lines in their meter, and the third in its simile, remember Sappho. Such information adds "nothing to the poem as object," much as "Drink to me only with thine eyes" gains nothing from the discovery (delayed till 1815) that it is made of sentences paraphrased from unimportant Greek prose. No one had thought to ask if it had a "source," so securely does it inhabit the English idiom. To wonder about "sources" is an aspect of wondering about Sincerity; we are inquiring whether the materials have received honest dealing.

Despite the attribution of two brief examples, no effort was under way to empedestal Reznikoff, who was dropped from later reprintings of the essay. "The degree of objectification in the work of Charles Reznikoff is small." "In contemporary writing, the poems of Ezra Pound alone possess objectification to a most constant degree; his objects are musical shapes." (This is to praise the self-sufficiency that was to keep the readership of *The Cantos* small until that beacon of sincerity, the Pisan sequence, seemed to redeem the enterprise. Such is public taste.) Objectification was also to be found in five poems of *Spring and All*, in two by Marianne Moore, in one by T. S. Eliot. Otherwise these writers stopped at Sincerity. The comment on Miss Moore is especially helpful in defining Zukofsky's meaning; her work "is largely a portrait of the author's character intent upon the presentation which is sincerity, rather than the revealed rest of objectification which is, for example, *An Octopus*." (Later her work would spatter Character like a dog shaking, to the delight of *Vogue* and *New Yorker* publics.)

Zukofsky's strategy was to plant a marker, "Sincerity," at a point the modern movement was widely understood to have reached, and then plant some distance away a second marker, "Objectification," to indicate a desirable direction of advance. These markers were more for the use of readers, critics and publicists than of poets. Poets, some of them, were achieving Objectification, some of the time, but so long as the quality went unnamed they were unlikely to receive credit for anything more than the Sincerity everyone could detect. This was the sincerity of Imagism ("direct treatment of the 'thing' whether subjective or objective"), the sincerity Hemingway advertised (" . . . to put down . . . what the actual things were which produced the emotion that you experienced"), the sincerity of the One True Sentence, unblurred by *a priori* notions of what written truth ought to be like. Being a moral quality mixed with a technical, it was congenial to American writers and aroused the subcutaneous religiosity of American readers, who confused this arousal with the emotions of Art. Objectification, as puritan in its formulations as in its exemplars, was a quality quite as profoundly American, though less stirringly so. Implying as it did a perfect indifference to any reader's approval, tending as it did to thrust arrangements of speech into the perfect thinghood of a snail shell (shaped, achieved, at rest), it comported with a latent sense that the arts ought not exhilarate, save austerely, and moreover that in a gray time (1931) they had best be gray.

Yet, unobtrusively, this newly stated criterion pointed toward a new order of achievement. Years later George Oppen spoke of having learned from Zukofsky "the necessity for forming a poem properly, for achieving form," and if "form" means the quiet that attends the achieved, the first poem in his *Discrete Series* (1934) is enviably formal:

> *The knowledge not of sorrow, you were*
> *saying, but of boredom*
> *Is—aside from reading speaking*
> *smoking—*
> *Of what, Maude Blessingbourne it was,*
> *wished to know when, having risen,*
> *"approached the window as if to see*
> *what really was going on";*
> *And saw rain falling, in the distance*
> *more slowly,*
> *The road clear from her past the window-*
> *glass—*
> *Of the world, weather-swept, with which*
> *one shares the century.*

Often young men affect to be quietly bitter, but not with

so geometric a refusal to raise the voice. The author of this was 21.

The Objectivists seem to have been born mature, not to say middle-aged. The quality of their very youthful work is that of men who have inherited a formed tradition: the tradition over the cradle of which, less than twenty years previously, Ezra Pound had hoped to have Henry James, O.M., speak a few sponsoring words. They are the best testimony to the strength of that tradition: to the fact that it had substance separable from the revolutionary high spirits of its launching. None of them makes as if to ignite bourgeois trousers. All that was history. They simply got on with their work.

The work frequently led into systems of small words. "The little words that I like so much," said Oppen, "like 'tree,' 'hill,' and so on, are I suppose just as much a taxonomy as the more elaborate words." This is important; it avoids Hemingway's implication that the small words have a more intrinsic honesty. It is cognate to Mallarmé's famous realization that nothing is producible of which we can say that "flower" is the name. ("I say, 'a flower,' and musically, out of oblivion, there arises the one that has eluded all bouquets.") That the word, not anything the word is tied to, is the only substantiality to be discovered in a poem gave Mallarmé ecstatic shivers; to command words' potencies was to oversee magic; to let them take the initiative was to set in motion glitterings "like a trail of fire upon precious stones." Oppen prefers to note that whatever words may be, men cannot survive without them. "They're categories, concepts, classes, things we invent for ourselves. Nevertheless, there are certain ones without which we really are unable to exist." Is the concept of humanity valid, he invites us to ask, or is it simply a "word"? "All the little nouns are the ones that I like the most, the deer, the sun, and so on. You say these perfectly little words and you're asserting that the sun is ninety-three million miles away, and that there is shade because of shadows, and more, who knows? It's a tremendous structure to have built out of a few small nouns. I do think they exist and it doesn't particularly embarrass me; it's certainly an act of faith. I do believe that consciousness exists and that it is consciousness of something. . . ."

This means that the little words depend on an act of faith as much as the big ones do. When Hemingway's Lieutenant Henry discovered for himself what has often been discovered, that nothing producible corresponds to abstract nouns, he hastens to make his separate peace and opt for physical pleasure with Catherine Barkley. But faith in the physical is also faith, as a society of hedonists would be held together by a belief in hedonism. We need not suppose that abstract nouns are empty whereas there is virtue in concrete ones. Rather, all nouns, all words, exist in a network of trust, and Frederic Henry has decided to trust no longer the network that runs through "glory," "courage," "honor."

Meanwhile, can we achieve something by agreeing that "deer" and "sun" have meaning, and "they" and "this" and "in" and "are"? Oppen achieved a "Psalm" with for epigraph "*Veritas sequitur . . .*":

> *In the small beauty of the forest*
> *The wild deer bedding down—*
> *That they are there!*
>
> > *Their eyes*
> *Effortless, the soft lips*
> *Nuzzle and the alien small teeth*
> *Tear at the grass*
>
> > *The roots of it*
> *Dangle from their mouths*
> *Scattering earth in the strange woods.*
> *They who are there.*
>
> > *Their paths*
> *Nibbled thru the fields, the leaves that shade them*

> *Hang in the distances*
> *Of sun*
>
> > *The small nouns*
> *Crying faith*
> *In this in which the wild deer*
> *Startle, and stare out.*

—A poem as bare as the street the sheriff walks, past the tied horses, past the bar, past the bank: the street that so nearly does not exist at all, indistinguishable from the wild plain but for board fronts that define it: boards the afternoon wind makes as if to level, and that shelter a few human rites maintained by common agreement, always evanescent. Like the Western camera, the Objectivist poet is the geometer of minima.

Zukofsky has worked since 1928 on "*A*," a long game of alertness to possibilities, single words floating loose to attach themselves to simultaneous contexts. The game commences at the top of the first page,

> *A*
> > *Round of fiddles playing Bach*

—where "A" is the title of the poem, and its first word (as of the alphabet), and the indefinite article, and the note musicians tune by. On page 70 Vitamin A enters the dance; on page 45, A-legged sawhorses that tumble as though weightless through an intricate juggling act, seven sonnets arranged like a canzone.

> *Horses: who will do it? out of manes? Words*
> *Will do it, out of manes, out of airs, but*
> *They have no manes, so there are no airs, birds*
> *Of words, from me to them no singing gut.*
> *For they have no eyes, for their legs are wood,*
> *For their stomachs are logs with print on them;*
> *Blood red, red lamps hang from necks or where could*
> *Be necks, two legs stand A, four together M.*
> *"Street closed" is what print says on their stomachs; . . .*

—Weightless, as in music, where there isn't a burden of

"meaning" and playing can seem like play. It's play that gets from sawhorses to manes to "out of manes, out of airs" by way of the Latin *manes* (ancestral spirits), and that ties "airs" to "words" ("I made it out of a mouthful of air," said Yeats) but also to tunes by way of "singing gut"—both the fiddle string and the insides wooden horses lack—and that gives "out of manes" the form of some such phrase as "out of gas." And these clumsy Pegasi serve not only for impoverishments (what's a Brooklyn poet got to work with?) but also for Renaissance emblems, since "two legs stand A," the name of the poem, and when four together make M they calligraph AM.

So rabbinical is the intentness of this difficult playing that it refuses to entertain questions about seriousness. Never mind that the materials are trivial. "A case can be made out for the poet giving some of his life to the use of the words *the* and *a*: both of which are weighted with as much epos and historical destiny as one man can perhaps resolve," so Zukofsky wrote in 1946. "Those who do not believe this are too sure that the little words mean nothing among so many other words." It's a curious possibility that the whole poem—over 600 pages so far, and still to finish—may be an exegesis of the indefinite article, and so of cases standing for kinds, and so of a tension between the kind of reality kinds have and the stubborn intuition that our need for a filing system has merely devised them.

> *I grant no one is deceived*
> *In so far as he perceives.*
> *The imaginations of the mind*
> > *in themselves*
> *Involve no error,*
> *But I deny that a man*
> > *affirms nothing*
> *In so far as he perceives—*
> > SPINOZA

And as to little words being weighted with history, we may

note Charles Williams' speculation (in his book *Witch-craft*) that the inability of a Latin devoid of articles to distinguish between "the" and "a" malign spirit may have hastened the conception of the devil: whence Salem.

An academic poetry? Hardly. The academy has consistently shunned it. Though the Objectivists were college men, though Zukofsky spent many years at college teaching, and though the New Criticism of the 1940's tended to be first and last something practiced by teachers, though Ph.D. candidates with New Critical supervisors scratched on their hands and knees for dissertation subjects, the Objectivists remained unnoticed, unreprinted, till the late 1960's. That is because, when the university network was linking up after the war, and taste for the first time was being made in classrooms, the prime criterion of poetic excellence was tending to become teachability, i.e. Nothing Too Subtle. "Paradox" and "Irony" became conjure words, and Geiger counters detected Concrete Imagery (Donne, Eliot) or noted a lack of it (Spenser, Shelley); I. A. Richards' tetrad, Sense, Feeling, Tone, Intention, was pillaged of one useful member, Tone (for Sense can be done without, and Feeling embarrasses adolescents, and Intention is very likely a fallacy); and Paradoxes of Tone amid Concrete Images were prodded at in a million freshman themes, written on one side only of the paper and with a wide margin (Canadian forests were leveled). It was a critical system sustained by the concurrence of very young minds which responded instantly to Prufrock (i.e. Sincerity) but had not enough experience of language or of one another's world to imagine that sincerity might be a first step, not a last. Poets—Pound and Williams notably—who offered no handle for such apparatus to hang on to where simply ignored, except as they had Ideas, and a kind of classroom poetry with concrete images and a salient tone you knew where you were with com-

menced to fill anthologies and magazines. The Academic
Poet wasn't a Zukofsky, but someone like Richard Wilbur:

> *A Ball will bounce, but less and less. It's not*
> *A light-hearted thing, resents its own resilience.*
> *Falling is what it loves, and the earth falls*
> *So in our hearts from brilliance,*
> *Settles and is forgot.*
> *It takes a skyblue juggler with five red balls*
>
> *To shake our gravity up. . . .*

That's a stanza to diagram; and, Miss Zworkyn, can you
name two things the poet means by "gravity"? Ah, very
good; and is there paradox in "light-hearted"? Mr. Kramp?
Yes, I think so too; and when you look ahead to the next
stanza you will find "spheres" and "heaven." Now, taking
those together with "gravity," Miss Carper . . . Of "The Red
Wheel Barrow" there just isn't enough to be said, nor of
the Zukofsky poem that observes as carefully as Hokusai
painted, and notes

> *Not the branches*
> *half in shadow*
>
> *But the length*
> *of each branch*
>
> *Half in shadow*
>
> *As if it had snowed*
> *on each upper half*

"Wit," then, "paradox," "irony," localized in key words to
be underlined on the blackboard, the other words so much
chalk dust to connect these loci. And lines are synthesized
out of "feet" (generally iambs, with substitutions), feet
out of words, the poem as though picked out by delicate
rifle shots, discrete, pocking the white expanse in array:

> *. . . pip Pop, pip Pop, pip Pop . . .*

—"Closed verse," said Charles Olson in 1950: "that verse which print bred and which is pretty much what we have had, in English & American, and have still got, despite the work of Pound & Williams." An historical vector in short, which fostered certain modes of contrivance, was being abetted by the college classroom, whose processes had a special predilection for verse so contrived. Education, which always tends to be packaging, handles with comparative ease the packet poem, whether the package intention ("This poem teaches us to persevere") or the package form, the sonnet, the ode: boxed in the poet's mind, then crated in lectures, then scattered into little square boxes for a multiple-choice exam. Assailing such crudities, the New Criticism offered subtler principles of packaging.

Which is not to be sniffy. America's intellectual destinies were always fated to be worked out in classrooms. Starting from scratch, the New World settlers had to import, after definite acts of choice, what in Europe had been simply environment. If there was a copy of Homer in Connecticut, it was because someone had decided to bring it along, or send for it. Yale University was founded on a gift of books. Curricula and reading-lists grow naturally out of such conditions: President Eliot's Five-Foot Shelf, for instance, or the Great Books, or the half-page list in Ezra Pound's "How to Read," which the *New York Herald Tribune* published in 1929. Probably no people in the world have given so much attention to determining the minimum essentials of culture. None, certainly, have endowed so many libraries, founded so many museums, printed so many books. And by the time, after World War II, when the college classroom was affecting nearly a majority of the college-age population, it was natural that the classroom should have begun to perform the functions of a Literary Establishment, determining what of all that had been written should receive deliberate attention. The next step was for something new to come out of a classroom; and a school of poets did.

The same Charles Olson who diagnosed "closed verse" supplied the next shaping of local energies. With perhaps in his mind some such analogy as the Chinese master whose calligraphed line will sway and thicken as the brush twirls and rises, one suave stroke through which a whole musculature flows, Olson proposed a "Projective Verse" responsive to the poet's breathing: a continuum, not a ratcheting.

If Olson's expositions seem messy it is because they are less composed than talked out; a classroom can be a place for talking things out, especially if there is no roster of "requirements" to be gotten through against a calendar, and the school non-accredited, making meaningless a calculus of grade points, and the non-accredited school moreover buried amid North Carolina hills, inaccessible save to the free-wheeling or the determined. It was from Black Mountain College, N.C., that the advance came: antibodies for academicism, from a rogue academy.

There was a *Black Mountain Review*, and there is an active generation of poets indebted to Olson's example and that of younger men—Robert Creeley, Joel Oppenheimer—who studied there under him. There is consequently a Black Mountain mystique, which need not concern us any more than its Bauhaus origins in the 1920's, nor the controversy whether the Olson incursion (late in the forties, after Josef Albers' departure) brought it to apotheosis or killed it. (Certainly it died in the fifties, from economic starvation; Olson was "Instructor and Rector" until 1956, and is said to have alienated the Quaker sponsors.)

It was a thrifty homemade campus, not cumbered with Gothic. From a Studies Building window, Fielding Dawson recalls, "you could see outside clear up the side of the mountain to the pasture where cows and chickens walked around." Classes ran to midnight sometimes, while "June bugs fell upside down wiggling on our books and papers."

These are not the standard campus memories. And Olson: "completely absorbed in his talk; the white blackboard began to fill with blue diagrams, blue words and long blue sentences, his hands turned blue and he had blue smudges on his face and mustache from smoking his cigar with his chalk hand, on he went, and once, with no place to write, he wrote towards the edge of the blackboard, wrote down the right margin, there was no right margin, but he went on, crossing over and going through already written sentences until he came to the chalk tray, and bending over, went clean off the blackboard to the floor, laughing with us." The Projective Verse essay in some ways resembles that white blackboard. He had taught at Harvard previously, and done something or other in Roosevelt's Washington. Six feet eight, perhaps, and he turned his shoulders sideways in passing through normal doors. The persona of his major work is named Maximus. "Behind his back we made jokes about him and whales." He says he once ate a polishing cloth.

> *(Trouble*
> *with the car. And for a buck*
> *they gave me*
> *what I found myself*
> *eating! A polishing*
> *cloth. And I went right on*
> *eating it, it was that good.*
> *And thick, color*
> *orange & black, with a nap. . . .*

Zukofsky wouldn't have done that.

And (Olson wrote, after talking it) the new poet must work in the open, "or what can also be called COMPOSITION BY FIELD, as opposed to inherited line, stanza, over-all form." He is a vector of energies, *pushed* from the moment he ventures into the open: "he can go by no track other than the one the poem under hand declares for itself." His ear registers minute identities, syllables; his breath generates shaped entities, lines. "And the line comes (I swear it) from the breath, from the breathing of the man who writes, at the moment that he writes, and thus is, it is here that, the daily work, the WORK, gets in, for only he, the man who writes, can declare, at every moment, the line its metric and its ending— where its breathing, shall come to, termination."

His expositions tend to sound like that, minute urgencies, stressed by commas, jabbing at the syntactic net. Paraphrase leaves little: an incantation for poets, a dowsing rod for readers. He does not, like Eliot, create new understanding; rather a Zeitgeist he profoundly sensed helps us understand him, its stammering oracle. Thus that a poem creates a field is a notion to rhyme with other mythologies of immersion, for instance the "acoustic space" of Marshall McLuhan, which is omni-directional so that one event cannot conceal another the way a penny in visual space can mask the sun. And Sound, an environment of modulated sound, was a craving of the fifties and sixties to which engineers responded busily, and still respond; thus dipping at random in a semi-technical magazine, we may find that "Stereo sound of all kinds, two-channel, three-channel, four-channel and beyond, gives us not just point source information (directionality) but random, ambient information which recreates our normal sonic experience." Then turning Olson's pages, we may read that

> *. . . the morning*
> *stands up straight, the night*
> *is blue from the full of the April moon*
>
> *iris and lilac, birds*
> *birds, yellow flowers*
> *white flowers, the Diesel*
> *does not let up dragging*
> *the plow*
>
> *   as the whippoorwill,*
> *the night's tractor, grinds*
> *his song*

—lilac and Diesel coequal parts of a world, not antagonists in some paradox.

Easy inclusiveness is his norm, as it is Whitman's. The contrast, though, is instructive. Whitman enacts what Zukofsky called Sincerity: that is, his own generous inclusiveness. Were he not so catholic a host, there would be no party. Marianne Moore enacts in the same way her *discriminating* inclusiveness, her poem a tidy guest list. Prior to the realized poem, Whitman means us to intuit the Poet, and Miss Moore an ideal Poem (her gridded field). The Olson field on the contrary, not gridded into counted stanzas, acknowledging no obligation to repeat and to ritualize, is also (until later Olson got self-conscious) devoid of a breezy presiding major-domo who waves aside such presuppositions. It is neutral; it is defined by what comes into it, syllables, lines.

> *The upshot is*
> *(and this the books did not tell us) the race*
> *does not advance, it is only*
> *better preserved*
>
>> *Now all lie*
>> *as Miss Harlow*
>>
>> *as Sunday supplement mammoths*
>> *in ice, as there used to be*
>> *waxworks*
>>
>> *as ugly as Jericho's*
>> *First Citizens, kept there*
>>
>> *as skulls, the pink semblance*
>>
>> *painted back on, as though they were once*
>> *and they were, Leaders*
>> *of the people*
>>
>> *with shells for eyes*
>>
>> *As she lies, all*
>> *white*

What makes a line a line is the interplay of syllabic detail; "as Sunday supplement mammoths" weaves a system of s's and m's; "waxworks" earns a separate line by being a phonetic curiosity, w/ks w/ks. The line can even assert enough sonoric efficacy to tug stress toward the second syllable of "Harlow"—

> *Now all lie*
> *as Miss Har Low*

—a nearly abstract chiming of syllables, disposed (Olson prized the typewriter) in typographic space. He needs a big page.

For all that it is shaped by breath, in typographic space the poem becomes an *object*, giving an unexpected twist to the formulae of the Objectivists. (The *collage* of the *Cantos* undergirds this principle also, open to prime Information, newspaper clippings, quotations. So does Williams' undertaking in *Paterson*, where we find guidebook excerpts and whole letters.) The achieved tranquillity the Objectivists stressed is a tranquillity proper to objects, things made, and such poems enter a world of things made, strange things, radial tires, lunar modules, combination locks, plastic bottles, disposable lighters, but not "aesthetic" things: not, for instance, statues. When Williams, about a decade after the Objectivist effort, called a poem "a machine made out of words," he was setting it in the field where America's prime energies have been expended ever since Henry Ford. The good life is no longer mocked by "the machine in the garden," the good life is realized by means of the machine: intelligence impressed on matter. It is a sentimental playing on little pipes for the poet to pretend otherwise.

Still, machines beget junk. Another of Olson's mortuary visions competes with the eleventh book of the *Odyssey* Pound has used to start the *Cantos* with—

> *and the rear tires*
> *were masses of rubber and thread variously clinging together*

as were the dead souls in the living room, gathered
about my mother, some of them taking care to pass
beneath the beam of the movie projector, some record
playing on the victrola, and all of them
desperate with the tawdriness of their life in hell

I turned to the young man on my right and asked, "How is it,
there?" And he begged me protestingly don't ask, we are poor
poor. And the whole room was suddenly posters and
          presentations
of brake linings and other automotive accessories, cardboard
displays, the dead roaming from one to another
as bored back in life as they are in hell, poor and doomed
to mere equipments . . .

A conjure object, a poem, to neutralize our psychic depend-
ence on objects. Moving with an anthropologist's detachment, the mind implied by such a poem would take in the
poem itself the kind of interest anthropologists take in the
objects whereby, they tell us, lost cultures have sought to
rhyme with the cosmos, and ritualize it, and ensure its con-
tinuance. Indeed poets turned anthropologists, turned outward toward lost cultures, native chants, old irrational wis-
doms—work of what one of them calls "The Technicians
of the Sacred"—have been part of the Olson legacy. He was
himself an amateur of Mayan and pre-Socratic vestiges:
another impress, perhaps, of the classroom, that force field,
where all is always now.

From amateur, Olson became impresario, and indulged in
a rhetoric not easily distinguished from bluff. We may
guess that in his later years, when his bear hug embraced
a vocation as itinerant campus catalyst, he spent too much
time talking to students who were too gladly impressed.
A poetry that had patrolled the very limits of coherence
commenced indulging itself in cosmic sweep—

          chained in being
          kept watch on by Aegean-
          O'Briareos whose exceeding

> *manhood (excellent manhood*
> *comeliness*
> *and power—100 or possibly*
> *to use the term of change (with*
> *the reciprocal 1/137 one of the two*
> *pure numbers out of which the world*
> *is constructed*
> > *(the other one is*
> *'Earth' mass mother milk cow body*
> *demonstrably, suddenly, more*
> *primitive and universal (?Hardly*

—and on and on: parentheses opening but never closing in a vertigo of Chinese boxes, a witty one-shot device become a mannerism, the poem a mastodon's floundering. A hundred books dipped into did service for one page ordered, and the poem's context came to be not the page but the campus reading, where as though to labor some obvious point about academic timidity, Olson turned incoherence into a style. Since his death in 1970 transcriptions of tapes have been printed like sacred oracles (". . . I also say that, as I say, a little to anticipate that difficult thing I propose to do, which is to read this poem, which as far as I know is un-understandable . . ."). He dredged riddling truths out of his dreams, welcomed questions but answered them with plosions of obfuscatory verbiage, and appeared to encourage confusion between his own ego and the time's collective unconscious.

> *Wholly absorbed*
> *into my own conduits to*
> *an inner nature or subterranean lake*
> *the depths or bounds of which I more and more*
> *explore and know more*
> *of, in that sense that other than that all else*
> *closes out and I tend further to fall into*
> *the Beloved Lake and I am blinder from*
>
> *spending time as insistently in and on*
> *this personal preserve from which*

> *what I do do emerges more well-known than*
> *other ways and other outside places which*
> *don't give as much and distract me from*

> *keeping my attentions as clear*

He became like the chameleon on the mirror in Gregory
Bateson's parable, bewildered in a universe of itself. The
world contains classrooms, invaluable subsystems; they do
not contain the world.

Publication, distribution—these continued in the forties and
fifties to present the usual problems. The capitalized firms
jumped in later, marketing offset reprints. Before their
advent Cid Corman had Zukofsky's "*A*" 1–12 manufactured
in Japan (a satisfying little hardbound, 296 pages, handset,
200 copies) and Jonathan Williams had the first *Maximus
Poems* printed (350 copies) in Stuttgart, where the big
pages that carry Olson's lines without runovers weren't
luxuries. You could buy "*A*" from Corman if you were so
fortunate as to be in touch with him, and *Maximus* from
Williams' Jargon Books if you were on the mailing list for
his encyclical letters. "Not to crowd you," runs a *Maximus*
detail,

> *not to crowd you. But what do we have*
> *but our wares?*

> *And who to market them to, things being*
> *how they are, but our friends?*

> *It has come to barter, it's got so*
> *primitive—like New England was,*
> *at its start . . .*

Later the Jargon/Corinth *Maximus* (1960), hand-sized,
entered, as hand-set folios could not, the college distribution
network. It is appointed to be read in seminars; likewise the
New Directions/City Lights Objectivist reprints (Oppen,
Reznikoff, Rakosi); likewise Zukofsky's *All* in two paper-

backs (Norton), likewise a paperback *Paterson* offset from
five hand-set limited editions, likewise such items as Robert
Creeley's *For Love* with a formal publisher's name on it,
after years of informal and improvised issuances.

Creeley, a student at Black Mountain and for seven
years editor of the *Black Mountain Review*, makes as if to
write a poem in a single act, like blowing a bubble. An early
and much quoted example, "I Know a Man," runs in its
entirety,

> *As I sd to my*
> *friend, because I am*
> *always talking,—John, I*
>
> *sd, which was not his*
> *name, the darkness sur-*
> *rounds us, what*
>
> *can we do against*
> *it, or else, shall we &*
> *why not, buy a goddamn big car,*
>
> *drive, he sd, for*
> *christ's sake, look*
> *out where yr going.*

So jauntily encompassing a Spenglerian darkness, this is an
instance of a new kind of poem. To look improvised, that is
the role, though we feel sure it is far from improvisation;
to look like a moment's thought, easy, light, and in thinking
it to swing like a high-wire walker. Or in Jonathan Williams' still jauntier formulation,

CREDO

> *I do*
> *dig Everything Swinging (thinking*
>
> *as I do:*
>
> *ah, art*
> *is fro-*
>
> *zen Zen)*

"Say it," wrote Williams, "no ideas but in things." And say it, no "poetry" but in poems. Wallace Stevens was the Last Romantic, the last poet of a long era that believed in "poetry," something special to be intuited before the words had been found, something of which one's intuition guided the precious words. "Is there any *poetry* here?" the Romantic reviewer would ask, looking up from the book; do I detect those harmonies that transcend the crass and the quotidian, that ignore the Ford car and the asphalt and the computer? No more. By the 1970's, thanks to a process that can be traced step by step for two generations from Pound and Williams, the American Poem is a new species of composition: the first new literary genre to have matured in the New World. (The Symbolist Poem, whatever Poe had to do with it, matured in France.) *The poem is the Gestalt of what it can assimilate*: so a new manifesto might run if there were need of manifestos; the Gestalt of what it can assimilate, like New York City; and a visitor to New York City at any time is apt to feel that the place is in process of being improvised. Structures run up, abandoned, left behind in a night; graffiti, sound and light shows, iridescences; neon; footnotes to history; registrations of the current, persistences in the memory, in tacit defiance of paperback transience: so the domain of the 1970's Muse.

For Oppen in *Seascape: Needle's Eye* (1972) the California coast suffices. One poem begins:

> *The sea and a crescent strip of beach*
> *Show between the service station and a deserted shack*
>
> *A creek drains thru the beach*
> *Forming a ditch*
> *There is a discarded super-market cart in the ditch*
> *That beach is the edge of a nation . . .*

Quite literally the edge, the western edge, and a camera could no doubt verify the other particulars. A skeptic would have little difficulty refuting anyone's insistence that the poet was assembling a metaphor. He depicts, surely, no more than the available world? And if his voice seems devoid of exhilaration, that may be simply because the available world is stark. Yet the poem, which has thirty-six more lines to run, does turn round on "edge," one of those little words. "The edge of a nation," as though the nation had fallen off the edge, leaving behind these mementoes for archaeology to ponder, or for poetry. We are soon to be reminded what war is going on beyond that edge and its ocean; and when, in a context of flying bullets,

> *The skull spins*
> *Empty of subject*
>
> *The hollow ego*
>
> *Flinching from the war's huge air*

we shall not know whether to locate that skull on a battle-field or on our own shoulders, nor which of the possible meanings to receive from "subject," from "hollow." If we do not hear the allegorist's voice uplifted, giving us cues to the meaningful and its way of meaning, that is thanks to Objectivism's "totality of perfect rest."

A structure of words, that's the aim, and the "meaning" is whatever applicability they attract. Oppen's "Song, the Winds of Downhill" can be about how to start writing poems again, or how to resume living now that there's no money, and it may be a first-person statement or a prophecy meant for all of us:

> *'out of poverty*
> *to begin*
>
> *again' impoverished*
>
> *of tone of pose that common*
> *wealth*
>
> *of parlance Who*
> *so poor the words*
>
> would   with   and   *take on substantial*

> *meaning   handholds   footholds*
>
> *to dig in one's heels   sliding*
>
> *hands and heels beyond the residential*
> *lots   the plots   it is a poem*
>
> *which may be sung*
> *may well be sung*

"Life begins above suburbia, but it's a hard climb," would be one way to travesty this. If the italicized "little words" are a poet's handholds and footholds, they are also (*would, with, and*) the operative concepts in a deprivation where all you've got consists of wishing and willing, comity, sequence. And if "tone" and "pose" are what language is impoverished of when we've worn out its rhetoric, they are also the substance of "that common wealth" affluence confers. "Plots" is a realtor's word and a cemetery salesman's word, also a *littérateur's* word. And what this poem amounts to "may well be sung" if we take it as a vision of some future after the machine has stopped. The hill-climbing is so barely there it's barely identifiable as a metaphor. Certainly the hill is no symbol; it's not even named save in the title, where "Downhill" seems merely to point the direction we're going. And certainly, though other hills and climbings appear in the collection, we'd be heavy-handed to refer to the ascent as the poet's Myth. It isn't climbing he'd have us interpret, but words. *No Myths* might be the Objectivist motto.

No Myths. It is here that Pound, the all-father, is left behind, and Williams, the Muse's obstetrician, looks as though he'd erred somewhat in his *Paterson* period. For Myths stand between facts and words. They are like "plots" and "statements" and even, lord help us, "messages": units of perception detachable from the language.

Thus Zukofsky dissents from those who have "raised up the word 'myth,' finding the lack of so-called 'myths' in our time a crisis the poet must overcome or die from." Since myths stand between facts and words, he is pleading for words that suffer no need of such intermediaries, being free-floating. Against such levitation the makers of syntactic boxes seek to legislate, but all they achieve is existence "entirely in that frozen realm without crisis that Dante called the 'secondary speech.' "

Myths stand between facts and words. Thus Pound in Canto II rehandles Ovid's myth of a kidnapped Dionysus who transformed his captors' ship into a rock and the captors into non-men. Pound's words give us the myth directly, taking its events as actual—

> *The back-swell now smooth in the rudder-chains,*
> *Black snout of a porpoise*
> > *where Lycabs had been,*
> *Fish-scales on the oarsmen.*
> > *And I worship.*
> *I have seen what I have seen.*

This "I" is both "E.P." and Ovid's Acoetes, addressing King Pentheus, who proposed to outlaw the revels; and Pound, by way of the myth, is both building his poem and addressing (yes he is!) the American Congress, which in 1919 had committed the Republic to what a much later Canto calls "the constriction of Bacchus." In Canto II no word mentions Congress; it is the myth, not the word, that reaches in many directions, including the direction of newspaper events, events it doesn't bring onto the page. The words stick to the business of rendering sensations, so that the myth, the radiant event, will be handed over to us actual. Then if we "interpret," we interpret the myth, as anthropologists did in the nineteenth century.

Which is a way to work, but not Williams' way, most of the time, nor Olson's, Oppen's, Creeley's. Conspicuously it is not Zukofsky's, whose interest in words as physiological gestures—things done with the breath and body—compelled his strange laborious version of Catullus, the intent of which is to force anyone who reads the English—

> *Irascibly iterating my iambics—*
> *unmerited, unique eh—imperator*

to breathe as did the poet who shaped the Latin—

> Irascere iterum meis iambis
> Immerentibus, unice imperator.

("I think there's a close relationship between families of languages, in this physiological sense. Something must have led the Greeks to say *hudor* and us to say *water*.")

So the structure of "*A*" is less like a sequence of themes than a sequence of word games, of which we are not told the rules. Some lie on the surface, as that "*A*" 12 is about as long as "*A*" 1–11 put together, or that "*A*" 14 is based on a progression of one-word, two-word and three-word lines. Others we happen to know about thanks to tips from the author; as that in reading aloud the opening of "*A*" 15 we are more or less pronouncing Hebrew passages from the Book of Job, or that the first half of "*A*" 9, five strophes and coda, in following precisely the rhyme scheme of Cavalcanti's "Donna Mi Prega" adapts from *Das Kapital* (Everyman edition) the phrases it sets to this tune, and moreover governs the distribution of "n" and "r" sounds according to the formula for a conic section. Who would think of counting the n's and r's? Yet the poet's "intention to have it fluoresce as it were in the light of seven centuries of interrelated thought" has chosen that rigorous and hidden way of impressing itself upon the language.

> *. . . Broken*
> *Mentors, unspoken wealth labor produces,*
> *Now loom as causes disposing our loci,*
> *The foci of production: things reflected*
> *As wills subjected; formed in the division*
> *Of labor, labor takes on our imprecision—*

Something, we could be sure without help, has interfered with the ordinary flow of discourse, and the language is responding not only to semantic sequence but to formal laws, though we cannot say unaided what those laws are. Musical laws in the same way, though we may not know what they are, yield effects we do not confuse with random sonority, which is what Zukofsky means us to understand in invoking so often the presiding spirit of Bach.

The purpose of reading "*A*" is not to discover its rules, only to explore the kind of linguistic experience that depends on awareness that hidden laws operate. In much the same way, a hidden law guarantees that the page you are reading now has more e's on it than h's. It is patterned by many such invisible force fields. If you were more aware of their tensions than prose permits, you would be reading a poem.

Take three instances. First, a memory of the poet's father:

> *"They sang this way in deep Russia"*
> *He'd say and carry the notes*
> *Recalling the years*
> *Fly. Where stemmed*
> *The Jew among strangers?*
> *As the hummingbird*
> *Can fly backwards*
> *Also forwards—*
> *How else could it keep going?*
> *Speech moved to sing*
> *To echo the stranger*
> *A tear in an eye*
> *The quick hand wiped off*
> *Casually:*
> *"I loved to hear them."*

"They sang this way"—we can hear the tune in those four words; and on another page we hear the heavy notes of the elders:

> *We prayed, Open, God, Gate of Psalmody,*
> *That our Psalms may reach but*
> *One shadow of Your light,*
> *That you may see a minute over our waywardness.*
> *Day You granted to Your seed, its promise, its Promise,*

> *Do not turn away Your sun.*
> *Let us rest here,*
> > *lightened*
> *Of our tongues, hands, feet, eyes, ears and hearts.*

And then their secularized children ("Deafen us, God, deafen us to their music") flout the Heritage, whoring after cosmopolitan beauties:

> *"Rain blows, light, on quiet water*
> *I watch the rings spread and travel*
> *Shimaunu-Sān, Samurai,*
> > *When will you come home?—*
> > *Shimauna-Sān, my clear star . . ."*

Three textures, three musics, moments in a poetic of continual measured change, change specifying its measure.

For did not all move in the poem we could not guess that laws were there, as without the moving water we could not discern the curled form of the waves, let alone compute their determining dynamics. Forms, many forms, grow out of the movement, what the words "say" only one of these. Something said can emerge as massive as a sheet of light; here he is in the fourth and fifth stanzas of "*A*" 11, addressing (like Cavalcanti) the song he is sending to his musician wife and violinist son, to flower for them when he is dead:

> *Graced, your heart in nothing less than in death, go—*
> *I, dust—raise the great hem of the extended*
> *World that nothing can leave; having had breath go*
> *Face my son, say: 'If your father offended*
> *You with mute wisdom, my words have not ended*
> *His second paradise where*
> *His love was in her eyes where*
> *They turn, quick for you two—sick*
> *Or gone cannot make music*
> *You set less than all. Honor*
>
> *His voice in me, the river's turn that finds the*
> *Grace in you, four notes first too full for talk, leaf*
> *Lighting stem, stems bound to the branch that binds the*

> *Tree, and then as from the same root we talk, leaf*
> *After leaf of your mind's music, page, walk leaf*
> *Over leaf of his thought, sounding*
> *His happiness: song sounding*
> *The grace that comes from knowing*
> *Things, her love our own showing*
> *Her love in all her honor.'*

This has not Eliot's way of echoing phrases and cadences, so we may not at first recognize the traditional Envoi: *Go litel boke.* "Raise," he instructs the song, "the great hem of the extended / World that nothing can leave," the world of pure music that is not the world I have relinquished but a world you (song) are capable of unveiling. This is the mirror of "his second paradise," where "his love was in her eyes."

Overwhelmed by the syntax (which patience can nevertheless penetrate), we may choose to content ourselves with the climate of musicality, an immediate delight as the quick movement incorporates run after run of rapid notes:

> *. . . leaf*
> *Lighting stem, stem bound to the branch that binds the*
> *Tree, and then as from the same root we talk . . .*

—from leaf down to the father's and son's common root, and their talk will be

> *After leaf of your mind's music, page, . . .*

"Page" elucidates "leaf" with perhaps a glance at Dante's leaves of the universe love has bound into a volume. "Page" is perhaps also one way the song is being enjoined to address the son, calling him by the title of a youth preparing for knighthood. And you, son, the song is to say, are to "walk leaf over leaf of his [the father's] thought," "sounding his happiness," apparently on your instrument, as from a score. And his happiness as you sound it will be a new song,

> *sounding*
> *The grace that comes from knowing*

> *Things, her love our own showing*
> *Her love in all her honor.*

Amid such intricacy, these are less things the words "say" than shadows they cast. Elsewhere Zukofsky lets what they "say" seem trivial. No matter; nothing is more ridiculous, if we close our ears, than what a violinist or a bassoonist does with his time and his fingers, and nothing more trivial than what goes into a poem (even the *Iliad*). A lit cigarette, a valentine, domestic anecdotes, even such details as

> *old*
>
> *Ez 1962*
> *1/29 in*
> The Times *crossword*
>
> *puzzle "Across/4*
> *Pound, poet"*

—each brings its quantum of attention or taut affection into the intricate *perpetuum mobile*. And as the collaborating mind of the listener alone justifies an Oistrakh's absurdly difficult stunt—scraping Bach's harmonies out of catgut— so in the minds of readers willing to let the poem teach them its appropriate modes of attention the forty-five years' enterprise called "*A*" hopes for its justification.

Collecting "meanings," sometimes, as casually as currents catch leaves, intently arranging its facets at other times to exchange reflected generations of meanings, this life's work of a prickly Brooklyn Jew who might have been born in Russia but for *pogroms*, and spent decades teaching young engineers to manage less clumsily a language he himself learned only after he'd learned Yiddish, this long intent eccentric unread game with its homemade rules seems as intensely indigenous an artifact as American ink and paper have ever transcribed.

VII ⁄ The Last Novelist

The Sound and the Fury (1929); it is permissible to dislike
it; there are things that are important beyond all this fedad-
dle. Reading it, however, with perfect contempt for it, one
discovers:

I ran down the hill in that vacuum of crickets like breath
travelling across a mirror. . . .

and

The shell was a speck now, the oars catching the sun in
spaced glints, as if the hull were winking itself along. . . .

and

. . . the last light supine and tranquil upon tideflats like pieces
of broken mirror. . . .

These are all from Part II, the monologue of Quentin
Compson, where the quotabilities swarm. The high finish

on the language of Quentin Compson (obit June 2, 1910, in Cambridge, Mass., by suicide [drowning]) suggests that he has, like Stephen Dedalus, "aesthetic" affiliations; sure enough, he is partly traceable to a drowned Pierrot in a one-act play, *Marionettes*, written by the undergraduate William Faulkner circa 1920.

In those years William Faulkner affected a cane and was nicknamed "The Count." He was writing imitations of Verlaine and Mallarmé and Austin Dobson, and drawing competent black-and-white designs that descend from Beardsley via Art Nouveau. The young folk in the drawings —rhythmically posed, toes pointed, faces afloat in consummate boredom—are the very dandies and flappers whose apotheosization by John Held, Jr., would later itself apotheosize the twenties. Seeing Faulkner's renderings next to Faulkner's poems of the same period, in the little posthumous book called *Early Prose and Poetry*, we cannot miss seeing how that particular line of American iconography stemmed from a British decadence by then twenty-five years gone: from *The Yellow Book*, say, and from rumors of *Under the Hill*. The naughty young folk of the twenties, the flaming youth by whom buyers of Horace Liveright books were so deliciously scandalized, played solemnly at an historical charade which they innocently ascribed to modern facilities, notably bathtub gin and Stutz roadsters, and Scott Fitzgerald's corresponding rhetoric—the moth, the pink dawn, the tuning fork struck on a star—uncannily recreates from blurred exemplars the vocabulary of Pierrot-and-Columbine poems he may not even have read.

Having a more orthodox literary sensibility than had Fitzgerald, Faulkner began writing with a clearer idea of the sources from which the American twenties were derived. In the year in which Fitzgerald was basing the rhetoric of *The Beautiful and Damned* on Compton Mackenzie and Michael Arlen (not to mention Mencken and Nathan),

Faulkner was making verse pastiches of the nineties which
Mackenzie and Arlen echo.

> *Columbine leans above the taper flame:*
> *Columbine flings a rose.*
> *She flings a severed hand at Pierrot's feet.*
>
> *Behind, a perpendicular wall of stars,*
> *Below, a gleam of snows.*
> *Pierrot spins and whirls, Pierrot is fleet;*
> *He whirls his hands like birds upon the moon. . . .*
>
> *Swift the wisps of motion blown across the moon;*
> *Columbine flings a paper rose,—*
> *Pierrot flits like a white moth on blue dark. . . .*

White moth, blue dark: Wallace Stevens fiddled with pretty
patterns like that, when he was finding ways to make his
language as arbitrary as he sensed it had to be. But Stevens
had no taste for the color of spilled blood this aestheticism
used to attract. Faulkner had. "She flings a severed hand at
Pierrot's feet": the Salome motif is detectable, and the
severed head of St. John as Mallarmé and Flaubert celebrated it, with for visual counterpart the bejeweled savagery
Gustave Moreau gave it in the painting that Mallarmé
prized. Faulkner's miscalled Mississippi Gothic is more
nearly a Mississippi aestheticism. The savageries his blood-
saturated rustics ritualize are of frozen Art Nouveau sump-
tuousness. The diction of his mature novels too keeps remembering these Art Nouveau beginnings.

> *When laggard March, a faun whose stampings ring*
> *And ripple the leaves with hiding: vain pursuit*
> *Of May's anticipated dryad, mute*
> *And yet unwombed of the moist flanks of spring . . .* [1925]

is comparable with

> There is the one fierce evening star, though almost at once
> the marching constellations mesh and gear and wheel strongly
> on. Blond too in that gathering last of light, she owns no dimen-
> sion against the lambent and undimensional grass. . . . [1940]

in its trick of playing verbal affinities across syntactic ones, so that we barely trouble to follow the syntax (in the poem it is not there to be followed) and receive the words in chewy gobbets: "unwombed of the moist flanks of spring"; "no dimension against the lambent and undimensional grass." This *impasto* of diction has affinities with *Symbolisme*, with for instance

> Mon doute, amas de nuit ancienne, s'achève
> En maint rameau subtil, qui, demeuré les vrais
> Bois mêmes, prouve, hélas! que bien seul je m'offrais
> Pour triomphe la faute idéale de roses.

—"L'Après-Midi d'un Faune," Mallarmé, 1876; and Faulkner's first published writing was a poem in the *New Republic* (August 6, 1919) called "L'Après-Midi d'un Faune."

Mallarmé's effort, he let readers of his prose understand, was toward simultaneity, the successive words dissociations of a chord. Some words in every language seem triumphantly expressive: *crimson* (to invent an English example), a sumptuous word for a sumptuous color. Others seem perfunctory: *red* shirks the simulation of blood and fire. And some words we may want are simply lacking: we must synthesize. Making up for these deficiencies, thought Mallarmé, the line of verse offers its rituals in place of poor semantic designations. Were the words right, as in Adam's legendary speech, we should have no need to compose, no need for the poet to appease that disquiet

> Dont le frisson final, dans sa voix seule, éveille
> Pour la Rose et le Lys le mystère d'un nom.

Faulkner took a similar view of the writer's obligations. When in 1962 an undergraduate asked him directly about his run-on sentences and chaotic pronoun references, he adduced the desire of any painter, writer, musician, to reduce all that he has experienced to "one single tone or color or word, which is impossible."

And the obscurity, the prolixity which you find in writers is simply that desire to put all that experience into one word. Then he has got to add another word, another word becomes a sentence, but he's still trying to get it into one unstopping whole —a paragraph or a page—before he finds a place to put a full stop.

"My ambition," he told Malcolm Cowley, "is to put everything into one sentence—not only the present but the whole past on which it depends and which keeps overtaking the present, second by second"—Mr. Faulkner, as he said in another connection, "trotting along behind" with paper and pencil.

A writer with ambitions of this order cannot but grow obsessed with ceaseless Time: the time that takes away syllables as they are uttered, eroding all possibility of that one polyvalent word; that consumes antecedent actions, compelling him to retrieve them by raids on the past; that consigns the vivid actual to myth; that segments and scatters and blurs and consumes all those lives, volitions, passions whose pressure on the momentary *now* lends it the meaning he sets out to capture—at what cost, in what serial stratagems. For the show of analysis, the show of syntax, are stratagems forced on the Symbolist by Time. Faulkner was neither an analytic nor a syntactic thinker, but a teaser into words, into sentences, paragraphs, chapters—all necessary, all unwelcome—of what was, to start with, a simple unverbalizable pulsating impulse.

On more than one occasion Eliot, another post-Symbolist, gave a not dissimilar account of how his poems were written. They began, he said, with a germinating *need*; the poet "does not know what he has to say until he has said it; and in the effort to say it he is not concerned with making other people understand anything. . . . He is going to all that trouble, not in order to communicate with anyone, but to gain relief from acute discomfort. . . ." This is a post-Symbolist embryology for post-Symbolist poems. Ben Jonson, who wrote out his sense in prose before finding verse, would have given a different account.

So Faulkner could recall after thirty-five years an aesthetic discomfort that commenced to alleviate itself as he visualized the muddy seat of a little girl's drawers: a "doomed little girl" climbing a pear tree to see a funeral: to see, more exactly, through the parlor window, "what in the world the grown people were doing that the children couldn't see." The ignorance of the muddy-seated little girl in the pear tree might effectively be redoubled, he supposed, by showing her "through the eyes of the idiot child who didn't even know, couldn't understand what was going on": death at a double remove of impercipience: an epiphanic moment suitable (he thought) for concentration onto a radiant pinhead, but apt to require in this imperfect world a few pages to get it all in. "I thought it was going to be a ten-page short story." Here is the germinal incident:

"Push me up, Versh." Caddy said.
"All right." Versh said. "You the one going to get whipped. I aint." He went and pushed Caddy up into the tree to the first limb. We watched the muddy bottom of her drawers. Then we couldn't see her. We could hear the tree thrashing.
"Mr. Jason said if you break that tree he whip you." Versh said.
"I'm going to tell on her too." Jason said.
The tree quit thrashing. We looked up into the still branches.
"What you seeing." Frony whispered.

This presents a scene but of course expresses nothing, since we do not know that it is death the house conceals. We need to know, and yet, by the Symbolist economy, we must not be told ("To name is to destroy," said Mallarmé.) We must gather it, then, from knowledges the children have. Thus they know that tonight authority is disrupted (" 'We've got

company.' Caddy said. 'Father said for us to mind me tonight.' "). The Negro children, moreover, Frony and Versh,
can know more than the white elders are allowing the white
children to know, and can let things slip. Frony asks,

> "Is they started the funeral yet."
> "What's a funeral." Jason said.
> "Didn't mammy tell you not to tell them." Versh said.
> "Where they moans." Frony said. "They moaned two days
> on Sis Beulah Clay." . . .
> "Oh." Caddy said, "That's niggers. White folks dont have
> funerals."
> "Mammy said us not to tell them, Frony." Versh said.
> "Tell them what." Caddy said. . . .
> "I like to know why not." Frony said. "White folks dies
> too. Your grandmammy dead as any nigger can get, I reckon."

We are to imagine that an idiot is recalling this, in an idiot's
eternal present. A work conceived as Faulkner conceived
his art could hardly not have generated an idiot. The idiot's
usefulness is that he can be supposed not to ask questions.
His mind is a timeless mosaic of pieces, not even remembered as normal minds remember, but all on one plane of
time, edge matching edge, associatively fitted. Questions
entail time, sequence, consequence, but epiphanic visions
disregard time. So it is in an idiot mind that the pieces
whose interlocking may make this epiphanic vision intelligible can be supposed to exist uninterrogated. The mind
of Benjy Compson is not a process, but a kind of *place* for
the elements of the story to exist in. We need not be surprised to learn that he isn't, in medical terms, a plausible
idiot, though a doctor writing in the *American Journal of
Mental Deficiency* took the trouble to find him "fabricated,"
"stuffed," in fact "literary." Of course he is literary; no
more than anything in literature is he a person. He is the
name of a principle on which some 20,000 words are organ-
ized: about 100 pages, having finished which, said Faulkner,
"I still hadn't told that story." The trouble with the idiot

consciousness, otherwise so attractive, is that the reader can hardly make head or tail of its lucubrations.

Continuing the account of his struggles with *The Sound and the Fury*, Faulkner dropped into the readiest convention of his later years, the tall tale: "So I chose another one of the children, let him try. That went for a hundred pages, and I still hadn't told that story. So I picked out the other one, the one that was nearest to what we call sane to see if maybe he could unravel the thing. He talked for a hundred pages, he hadn't told it, then I let Faulkner try it for a hundred pages. And when I got done, it still wasn't finished" (though anyway it was published, 400 pages of it) "and so twenty years later I wrote an appendix to it, tried to tell that story."

He was a born storyteller, and this is itself a funny story: the future Nobel laureate struggling against hope, against language, against the grain of fiction, against the very nature of things, to show us nothing more than a child with muddy drawers peeping at a funeral, and not succeeding, not after two decades. It is myth; we are not to believe it; and yet it contains exegetical truth, displaying what forced him to make *The Sound and the Fury* so complicated. "That's all I was doing on the first page," he stated, "trying to tell what seemed to me a beautiful and tragic story of that doomed little girl climbing the pear tree to see the funeral." Yet it's an incident most readers will barely remember, the weight of the narrative having shifted so massively toward exegesis of that exact word "doomed." It is only because Caddy is "doomed" that her rearward aspect in the pear tree is "beautiful and tragic," and spinning the threads that will render her doom intelligible came to occupy most of the novel's space.

Her doom, as it proved, was not to be wholly specified until the 1945 Appendix, where we learn how Caddy's fortunes leaped not only out of the 1929 book but clear out of any conceivable circle of consciousness the 1929 book could have contained. Her trajectory brought her ("ageless and beautiful, cold serene and damned") to the shining car, and implicitly the bed, of a German staffgeneral in occupied France: this, for a Mississippi Compson, a bitter, defiant, compounded harlotry: willed doom. In the 1929 novel she has simply been gone since 1911, when, cast off by her Indiana husband, she left her child (not his) at her family home and departed. True to the Symbolist principle of indirection, the novel concentrates on the doom of the child, from which we infer the scale of Caddy's doom. The novel, in fact, occupies itself with the child—no, it doesn't; she barely appears until it's more than half over. Start again. The novel, in fact, comes to theoretical focus around the child's decisive act of rebellion; for on April 8th of 1928 the child, named Quentin after her drowned uncle, "swung herself by a rainpipe from the window of the room in which her [other] uncle had locked her at noon" to the window of the uncle's bedroom, where she stole nearly $7,000 and "climbed down the same rainpipe in the dusk and ran away with the pitchman who was already under sentence for bigamy. And so vanished. . . ."

But wait, that's wrong too, though the wording is Faulkner's from the 1945 Appendix. The writer of the 1929 novel had specified several times that Miss Quentin climbed down the pear tree, the same in which her mother had sat with muddy drawers, and moreover had used it in the manner of the "Merchant's Tale": a mechanical allegory, this, which he himself forgot before Malcolm Cowley's enthusiasm for the coherence of the Yoknapatawpha Saga had spurred him to this piece of incoherence.

Let that pass. The novel (we were saying) comes to theoretical focus on this act of Miss Quentin's, because the idiot Benjy's monologue (Part I) is dated the day of the evening Miss Quentin went down the pear tree (or rainpipe), and incorporates ancillary glimpses we can't at that stage decipher—Miss Quentin in the swing with a vulgar fellow (*"They sat up in the swing quick. Quentin had her hands on her hair. He had a red tie."*), Miss Quentin spatting with her uncle Jason (*"I hate this house. I'm going to run away."*); moreover because uncle Jason's monologue (Part III) is dated the day before that, and details his effort to take charge of her, and his new policy of locking her up; and lastly because the final narrative (Part IV) begins on the morning after, when her absence is discovered and all hell breaks loose. So insofar as our impulse as we read is to make out what is happening in the novel, what we make out is Miss Quentin's flight.

Yet the flight is unimportant, just as Quentin herself is unimportant: a slatternly rebelliousness, thinly characterized. Though she does do something explicit, she is a peripheral character, really; a means for making known to us the estrangement, long before, of her mother, Caddy, whom Faulkner first thought of as a little girl with muddy drawers, aloft in a pear tree. Quentin's promiscuity re-enacts Caddy's (and the idiot's glimpse of Quentin necking in a swing is confused, in a way rereading will only partly disentangle, with a similar earlier glimpse of Caddy). Quentin's flight with a carnival pitchman re-enacts Caddy's flight, the one that took her to a movie magnate's bed and later to a Nazi officer's. The rough-cast saliences, these are the things a good Symbolist avoids dwelling on: rather their torques, their eddies, their reflections. The doom of the doomed little girl, which is what all this started with, the doomed little girl in the tree, we glimpse refracted through the cheaper doom of her daughter, and through the exacerbations of the brother who was closest to her, the brother for whom she named that daughter, the brother who drowned himself in 1910 after spending the day we spend with him in Part II, where much poetry of death does not really declare his termination, any more than his incest with Caddy is declared. And the suicide, we understand at last, did occur, but the incest did not; Quentin consummated only one of the two violences that haunted him. (Only the Appendix really settles—if it does—the question whether the incestuous liaison of Quentin with Caddy occurred or not.)

What Quentin did do, when his sister gave herself to a lover, was offer to kill her; he held a knife to her throat, but somehow dropped it. She had thrown herself supine in shallow water, "her head on the sand spit the water flowing about her hips . . . her skirt half saturated," and with the knife at her throat Quentin remembered her earlier violation by muddy water:

> do you remember the day damuddy died when you sat down in the water in your drawers
> yes
> I held the point of the knife at her throat . . .

—Those muddy drawers again: a *leitmotif*. The day damuddy (grandmother) died she had muddied them out of willfulness. There is willfulness, too, in the saturated skirt today, the day she was violated (and let herself be). A symbol, then, of the degraded woman of the house of Compson? Rather, a piece of pathos on the earlier occasion, a novelist's linking device on the later. You haven't got time, Faulkner told a questioner, to be thinking about images and symbols. You've got all you can manage without that. Writing a novel, he said, is like trying to nail together a henhouse in a hurricane.

Faulkner's "symbols" have been talked about as loosely as those of his first mentors, the Symbolists, who used symbols seldom. The fault is as much his as anyone's. Nailing his henhouse of the moment together, he let matching knotholes guide his choice of boards, or remembered details from distinguished architects. When Caddy (on page 234) is reminded that her paw told her to stay out of that tree, and rejoins that that was a long time ago, we cannot put aside the thought that Faulkner has remembered something similar from the book of Genesis, without taking time (since the tree became a rainpipe later) to decide how seriously he meant us to dwell on the parallel. A Symbolist poem, like an ideal Faulkner novel—one of the archetypes we shall maybe read in Heaven—elaborates verbal formulae, verbal interactions, creating a world dense with specificity but difficult to specify. (The tree Caddy's paw told her to stay out of is just at that moment insufficiently verbal; it looms up, an Edenic allegory.) The Symbolist work, avoiding symbols, prolongs what it cannot find a way to state with concision, prolongs it until, ringed and riddled with nuance, it is virtually camouflaged by patterns of circumstance. (You cannot skim a Faulkner story.) With good will, an identifiable world emerges, which, seeing the lavish trouble the writer has taken, we are apt to try to "interpret." This is usually a mistake. It is a mistake to exclaim portentously over Caddy's muddied drawers, or to see the Doom of the Old South in the decline of the Compsons (though Faulkner himself, in ill-considered moments, spurs us on). Readers who want to see the Doom of the Old South in everything Faulkner contrived are indulging, probably, extra-literary satisfactions. He shows no special sign of thinking the Old South more doomed than any other sector of humanity. It was simply the sector he knew. The reader's desire to find symbols derives from the desire to interpret, which in turn is apt to be linked to the desire to be horrified by epiphanic goings-on in a region where one congratulates oneself on not living. Shakespeare's groundlings thought of Italy thus. *Mais la lecture ne peut pas y consister.*

For Faulkner's root need was not to symbolize (a condensing device) but to expand, expand: to commence with the merest glimpse and by way of wringing out its significance arrange voices and viewpoints, interpolate past chronicles, account for just this passion in just this ancillary passion, and tie the persons together, for the sake of intimacy, intensity, plausibility, with ties of blood and community and heritage.

Those, not the "symbols," are Faulkner's real ties. One can guess, for instance, what made him spatch in that Edenic allusion. He meant it not for a real allegory, but as notation for the child's puzzled attempt to understand what Death is, something portentous. All is portentous; all, in his sense of things (which was not Cartesian), must reach vaguely beyond itself. The fiction writer's plots, by emphasizing linkage and fit, tend to conceal that reach, which helps explain Faulkner's efforts to submerge his plots, sometimes in their own intricacies. He needed linkages that were not causal, that did not resemble the internal linkages of machines. What the Old South gave him, what is inseparable from his preferred way of working, making possible in fiction what is essentially a method for poetry, was a society of which he could plausibly postulate that everything in it affects everyone. He needed inarticulate blood ties. When he relaxed his reliance on the Old South, and tried instead (see *A Fable*) to project Significance with the help of Allegory, the result is dreadful. A parallel between 1918 events and events traditionally dated 33 A.D. was something his method simply could not assimilate. (What method could is a question we needn't face; but the bewilderment *A Fable*'s failure occasioned tells us something about the critics' misunderstanding of his method.)

And as no Faulkner incident can yield its significance until it has entangled circumambient lives and circumstances even to the third and fourth generations, so no Faulkner novel really cuts off at its boundaries. Characters pass from one to another, a story illuminates the early history of a family we will later meet in a novel, people in a new book serve as analogues and reflectors for other people the author conceived years previously. Jason Compson (*The Sound and the Fury*, 1929) is nowhere more devastatingly "located" than by the sentence (Appendix, 1945) that tells us he "competed and held his own with the Snopeses." The Snopeses, who run through Faulkner country like a geological fault (they "took over the little town following the turn of the century as the Compsons and Sartorises and their ilk faded from it"), came late into his chronicles if only because a man must do one thing at a time; though Flem Snopes is mentioned in *Sartoris* (1929), their full and manic proliferation commences only with *The Hamlet* (1940), which in turn grew out of the story called "Spotted Horses" (1932). When Malcolm Cowley first pointed out in 1945 how the Faulkner books interlock, nine of them were still to appear; ideally we should have his entire work before us at once, including—also, alas, ideally—the books he would have written in a second lifetime; which is only to say that his work was impossible to finish, and even, in detail, impossible to accomplish. God himself has not yet stopped.

As years went by, the vast interdependent *oeuvre* came to seem like a feat of planning, though it was more like a marathon improvisation. And the convention toward which his fictions approximated, retreating from the highly "literary" convention of *The Sound and the Fury*, a book written by a man who had just read *Ulysses*, was that of the tall tale spun on a timeless afternoon.

In having all time at his garrulous disposal, the tale-teller is the next best thing to an idiot, and considerably more amenable to fiction. He needs no sense of proportion; he need not foreshorten; he can dilate, he can expatiate, he can make us grasp by sheer explicitness all that was so wonderful about the bare anecdote, filling in meditations, preliminaries, relationships. He can assume, moreover, that he need not think about how to perform the most troublesome of all the novelist's tasks, which is "introducing" characters, for we and he, our feet together at a wooden railing, know the town, know the families, know without being told those things the conventional novelist must be at pains to plant and develop and imply: who is whose cousin, who is whose natural father; who is rumored to carry Negro blood, whose fortunes despite appearance were long ago lost, whose brother rattles the bars of what remote jail.

> . . . this was not something participated in or even seen by himself, but by his elder cousin, McCaslin Edmonds, grandson of Isaac's father's sister and so descended by the distaff, yet notwithstanding the inheritor, and in his time the bequestor, of that which some had thought then and some still thought should have been Isaac's, since his was the name in which the title to the land had first been granted from the Indian patent and which some of the descendants of his father's slaves still bore in the land. . . .

"That which some had thought then and some still thought" isn't taleteller's speech—the quotation is from the formal overture to *Go Down, Moses*—but it uses as its convention the taleteller's attitude: that everyone knows these genealogies and these lines of inheritance, that from inside the community of taleteller and listeners they are not at all labyrinthine. Manipulating this convention, Faulkner can give us past deeds in a hieratic idiom, like that one, or in a colloquial idiom, like this one:

> And after that, not nothing to do until morning except to stay close enough where Henry can call her until it's light enough to chop the wood to cook breakfast and then help Mrs. Littlejohn wash the dishes and make the beds and sweep while watching the road. Because likely any time now Flem Snopes will get back from wherever he has been since the auction, which of course is to town naturally to see about his cousin that's got into a little legal trouble and so get that five dollars. 'Only maybe he won't give it back to me,' she says, and maybe that's what Mr. Littlejohn thought too, because she never said nothing. . . .

By the standards of *Madame Bovary* or of *Dubliners* or, for that matter, of *Tender Is the Night*, this is a miserable narrative technique. The lines of action do not stand clear at all. By the standards of local gossip it is phonographic realism. And by the standards of the kind of fiction Faulkner worked out over many years, it is vivid and funny provided you have learned to pay, in many preceding pages, the kind of attention by which you get the hang of the community almost like a native, and intuit the proper vectors when a name like "Flem Snopes" is simply mentioned.

But notice what has happened now. Out of its sheer need to keep spinning out circumstances, the arty mode of narration we encountered in *The Sound and the Fury* has in a very few years discovered a convention that makes it look artless. It is like the way Cubist drawings people thought "any child could do" evolved from an accomplished mode of portraiture that happened to contain within it the ambition to analyze space. The route the artist travels, that is what counts; and Faulkner came to the folk tale in a new way, which was not, for example, the *faux naïf* way of Sherwood Anderson.

The consequence is important to understand. Faulkner discovered, whether by cerebration or by trial and error, that the Symbolist expansion of an incident, provided we imagine the incident in a real world and not in an art-world like that of Mallarmé's *Igitur*, expands it into a kind of unbounded interrelatedness, the kind taletellers count on everyone knowing. The Symbolist's ideal timelessness becomes the taleteller's ideal leisure. Faulkner could therefore use the taleteller's convention as a natural expansion of the Symbolist's convention; could use it, even, to go on with a vast tapestry in which "Symbolist" fiction like *The Sound and the Fury* also figured, so that *The Sound and the Fury* comes to seem not a false start within the oeuvre but an integral part of it. And to this method Flaubert's kind of fiction, and Joyce's and Conrad's, the kind of fiction that underlay *The Sound and the Fury*, comes to seem irrelevant, since their well-made fiction postulates a self-contained artifact, bounded, integral.

Integritas, Stephen Dedalus thought, is the first thing we perceive, the self-sufficiency of the work before us; *consonantia* next, the interrelation of its parts (like those of a "machine made out of words") and lastly *claritas*, the radiant affirmation. But Faulkner seems not to care for such Grecian-urn criteria. A story, in his usage, was a unit of attention within the large *oeuvre*. The stories in *Go Down, Moses* make up a chronological panorama, the fine "Delta Autumn" not really intelligible without its five predecessors, and "The Fire and the Hearth" completed in curious ways by a different book altogether, by no means one of his best yet irreplaceable, *Intruder in the Dust*.

From nearly total neglect in the early 1940's, Faulkner by the 1960's had risen in critical esteem to the rank of major novelist. This happened in part because he was "ahead of his time," which means that a change in the assumptions of fiction occurred earlier in his work than it occurred in the mind of the reading public. His development, in short, was paradigmatic: a development that left the "closed" novel behind. The self-sufficient information machine, coextensive with its physical package, the equilibrium of geodesic forces *Ulysses* apotheosized, had become by the 1960's an elaborate practical joke, a strange end for the dominant literary form of nearly a hundred years.

Conrad and Ford Madox Ford and Joyce, all their generation in modernism's heroic age, had struggled to replace what seemed to them scribbled fiction with something both more artful and more real. (There was a time when *Ulysses* seemed raw life.) Their craft remains unimpugnable, but their image of life is no longer as plausible as it was. As assumptions neither he nor his readers were aware he was making now cause the work of the Victorian novelist to look "Victorian," so other assumptions of which no one was aware now stamp the enclosed fiction as the product of a time for which we do not yet have a label. One of these may have been the synecdochic assumption, the assumption that the part is eloquent of the whole, the remark of the mind, the behavioral tic of the person, so that the artist is an artisan of signifying parts, and the aesthetic whole a pre-established nestling of significances. Hence its cross-references; hence its ideal suitability to exegesis; and Joycean scholarship has virtually become part of Joyce's text. It is not surprising that the scholar became an absurdity, and the sleuth-eyed reader the butt of fictional jokes. So that great bounded work, with nestled within it all that might be required to minister to its understanding, the artifact in typographic space on the margins of which penciled notes could accumulate: this pantechnicon, this well-packed Ark, this (in Karl Shapiro's phrase) cuckoo clock of literature, is today, along with the scholarship it entails, a vehicle for erudite humor. When Nabokov's *Pale Fire* was greeted as a masterpiece the criteria of the "closed" novel were becoming absurd. How well *Pale Fire* answered to those criteria!—a novel's thousands of pieces shuffled and arranged, without loss of cohesion, to yield a 999-line poem and an obsessed commentator's 200 pages of scholarship. "It is one of the very great works of art of this century," said one of the century's more emphatic critics. But *Pale Fire* is a mirthless hoax and so is its successor, *Ada, or Ardor*: ingenious ships-in-bottles riding plastic seas to the awe of teaching assistants. Less vindictively hollow, Thomas Pynchon's *V*, amid its intricate promise of significances it is careful never to deliver, proclaims that all the world's a comic book. The big books that make a game of soliciting our note cards are mocked in John Barth's *Giles Goat-Boy*, which itself makes a hollow game of having been machine-written from computer cards. Barth next puts in a personal appearance ("bald as a roc's egg") in *Chimera*, to explain to his two newest characters that he's at an impasse. "My name's just a jumble of letters; so's the whole body of literature: strings of letters and empty spaces, like a code that I've lost the key to." Strings of letters and empty spaces: much as the "classic" detective novel, that puzzle box, has died utterly away, the big book full of Piranesi corridors now insists on its own illusoriness, and fades.

And with it goes the sense of life it fostered: the dialogue exactly heard, honed, polished; the absolute scientific typicality that stemmed from Flaubert's notebooks where he wrote down what people *always* said, and that got arranged according to Ford's conviction that since people never listen to other people, a conversation in a novel should be a fugue of purposeful cross-purposes. The writing schools have taught these wiles so well they now seem formulaic.

Was Faulkner, perhaps, the Last Novelist? His was our last mutation, anyhow, of the procedures that dominated the novel for many decades. They stemmed from the nineteenth century's confident positivism, from the belief that what was *so* was the writer's province, that he was the supreme generalist, to be trusted by the literate for the reports they needed. Though only writers seem to have held that belief in their own social utility, still it was the belief from which they wrote. ("To forge," wrote Stephen Dedalus, "in the smithy of my soul the uncreated conscience of my race.") The serious artist, Ezra Pound used to argue (recapitulating assertions he heard from Ford), has the obligation faithfully to mirror our folkways (*Moeurs de Province*, Flaubert subtitled *Madame Bovary*) since otherwise we shall not know what they are. Our health depends on his reports, as much as on a hospital technician's. And *Ulysses*, Pound thought, was the lancing of a boil. Such polemics derive from Flaubert's reported remark that if "they" had read *L'Éducation Sentimentale* the war of 1870 would not have happened. We can no longer think so. Then what are words for anyway?

If that is the kind of question we ask now, in part it is because the American Modernists did their work thoroughly. A "movement" begins by stating, not always formally, what the set of available possibilities is, and then seems to exhaust the set. There ensue cries about the Death of Art, until a new set has been discovered. To today's ears, those cries are familiar.

So what was the field of possibilities that got worked out? Its key assumption was one peculiarly adapted to America's sense of reality. It is an assumption about Language, the one topic of passionate concern to everyone involved in the enterprise: the one thing we can imagine Miss Moore, for example, discussing with Hemingway. The assumption is that Language is something arbitrary, something *external* both to the speakers who use it and to the phenomena they hope to denote. Its norms are not imposed by history, they are elected, and if they turn out to be misleading us we can elect new ones. Frederic Henry is doing something like that when he equates such words as "sacred," "glory" and "sacrifice" with discredited politicians.

That a language may be less a heritage than a code, and a code moreover that we are free to change, has been suspected in other times and places, but never so much as in America has it been felt in a whole people's bones.

T. S. Eliot felt it in his bones and tried to flee it, holding as he did other beliefs incompatible with it. Eliot cherished "the historical sense," and thought that a poet's most individual moments might be those when "the dead poets, his ancestors" were asserting themselves most vigorously. When he wrote that "a ceaseless care, a passionate and untiring devotion to language, is the first conscious concern of the poet," he was careful to specify two duties this care imposed: "Study of how his language has been written, in both prose and verse, in the past, and sensitiveness to the merits and shortcomings of the way in which it is spoken and written in his own time."

That is to see the language as a principle of civilized continuity, in which it behooves the writer to immerse himself with devout self-abnegation. Stubbornly submissive to the democracy of the dead, acute about today's demotic shortcomings, the writer whom Eliot imagines stirs a latency called Tradition, of greater authority than he. Its resonances enhance his voice.

But that was just where Williams perceived no enhancement, only "words hung with the pleasing wraiths of former masteries." No, words (for Williams) needed to be "separated out by science, treated with acid to remove the smudges, washed, dried and placed right side up on a clean surface." *The Waste Land* was not written in that way, nor *In Memoriam*, nor *Heart of Darkness*. But Williams said that it was how Marianne Moore's poems were written, and it was moreover an ideal he proposed for himself. It was how he wrote "The Red Wheelbarrow,"

> *a red wheel*
> *barrow,*

"red" beside "wheel" and "barrow" under both. And we have seen how the words in that poem are moved to some zone where we need not imagine somebody speaking them. Speech is external to speakers.

Laid "right side up on a clean surface," words may interact in fascinating ways. Thus "red" is an adjective. In this arrangement, does it modify "wheel"? It seems to. But "wheel" is itself a kind of adjective modifying "barrow," and "red" moreover, in spoken usage which is somehow pertinent, attaches itself to "wheelbarrow," a word not really present in the poem. Such interactions seem to require mathematical treatment: one can imagine a diagram for their composition of forces, holding the little pattern in equilibrium.

These interactions, whose minute energies help make the poem interesting, can occur once we have partially separated "wheel" from "barrow": that is, once we permit the language to exist on two simultaneous planes: the plane of usage, the plane of words "separated out by science." On the one plane they "denote," more or less; on the other they make patterns, and these two operations do not interfere with one another. They do interfere with the way a reader receives a meaning, offering him so many conflicting cues to attend to at once, and if he does learn to take pleasure it's in that omnidirectional vigilance, like a frontier scout's.

Separate its elements out by science (which may mean, by typewriter) and the simplest sentence commands an exhilarating openness of attention. Try a detail from Marianne Moore's "Virginia Britannia:"

> *Rare*
> *unscent-*
> *ed, provident-*
> *ly hot, too sweet, inconsistent flower-bed! Old Dominion*

—three stepwise polysyllables saying "-ent," the middle one with a different grammar from its outflankers; and has "inconsistent" ever before found itself next to "flower-bed"? As for the "Old Dominion," it seems appositively placed, which would equate it with the flower-bed, though as we read on it turns out to be a compound epithet for the first word in the next stanza, which is "flowers."

Such poems resemble the games Erik Satie and Charles Ives at different times played with their calligraphed scores, making visual patterns you can't hear to counterpart the music's patterns you can't see. Or they are reminiscent of an at-homeness with computer codes: the intricate adaptation of the information at hand to the rules of a field and the internal logic of a machine that is uninterested in information. Or they come to language as Thoreau came to Nature, not as pupil to Wordsworth's wise teacher but as the Inspector of Sunsets, the vigilant scrutinizer of phenomena he wouldn't know how to predict.

When I began to cut holes for sounding there were three or four inches of water on the ice under a deep snow which had sunk it thus far; but the water began immediately to run into these holes, and continued to run for two days in deep streams, which wore away the ice on every side, and contributed essentially, if not mainly, to dry the surface of the pond; for, as the water ran in, it raised and floated the ice. This was somewhat like cutting a hole in the bottom of a ship to let the water out. When such holes freeze, and a rain succeeds, and finally a new freezing forms a fresh smooth ice over all, it is beautifully mottled internally by dark figures, shaped somewhat like a spider's web, what you may call ice rosettes, produced by the channels worn by the water flowing from all sides to a centre. Sometimes, also, when the ice was covered with shallow puddles, I saw a double shadow of myself, one standing on the head of the other, one on the ice, the other on the trees or hillside.

You never know what you are going to find at the next look, nor in the next sentence. So the energy William Carlos Williams, for one, celebrated in poem after poem is felt by the reader as a tiptoe readiness for the next minute verbal surprise.

> ... It should
>
> be a song—made of
> particulars, wasps,
> a gentian—something
> immediate, open
>
> scissors ...

Readiness is all.

The new language (new to each user) is like the new world. You never know what you are going to find. (Nor did

Jimmy Gatz, though he knew that one condition of finding was to give his name as Jay Gatsby.) Into Zukofsky's long poem goes a *mot* of his little son's, that if you aren't careful in the woods—Fenimore Cooper is paying attention—you may

> *Slip gerplump*
> *On a stump;*

also on a neighboring page a clergyman's misspelling,

> Merditations;

also a clipping on the curiosities of English:

> *A sege of herons*
> *A spring of teals*
> *A bevy of quails*
> *A gaggle of geese*
> *A covert of coots. . . .*

This delight in what the language throws up isn't like the delight we take in Joyce's virtuosity, which we ascribe not to impersonal possibility but to a unique man's resourcefulness. The American tradition—look at *Moby Dick*—is to offer discoveries, not virtuoso performances. As great a virtuoso as America can show in this century was Wallace Stevens, and his virtuosity unlike Joyce's was a willingness to display linguistic possibilities no one, least of all Stevens, could have "thought of." He could (and Joyce could not) write "nonsense," which requires more attention in a way than does sense. "The Woman Who Blamed Life on a Spaniard": there is no procedure for thinking of a title like that. You find it by turning over stones.

So styles are not obliged, not by decorum, not by tradition, not even in Wallace Stevens, who appears to be using a traditional blank-verse style. Styles are *elected*. Hemingway elected his, uncoerced by the dead writers his ancestors. Rules are made up *ad hoc*. They may be intricate. They need not be "historical." Stevens put blank-verse lines into a three-line unrhymed stanza of which it would have been difficult to foresee a use until Stevens had used it many times. Miss Moore designed intricate syllabic shapes. Thus "Virginia Britannia" is made of 12 stanzas each of 12 lines, their syllable count 7, 10, 11, 12, 8, 12, 5, 13, 12, 6, 4, 14, and with lines 3, 7 and 12 rhyming, also lines 4, 5, 6, also lines 10 and 11. She had not used this pattern before, and having taken the trouble to invent it did not use it again. Or the rule may be like Hemingway's: short words, declarative sentences, conjunctions preferable to semicolons. Or it may after all be a rule discovered in history, but separated from historical circumstance. Pound and Eliot both wrote sestinas, Pound in a poem that begins "Damn it all," and Eliot in a celebration of Gloucester (Mass.) fishermen. Dante, whose explanation of the sestina is the one that has come down to us, would have found both these uses inexplicable.

The New World felt itself detached from European necessities. Two millennia's resources are simply available, for free election. Moreover, one may make up more.

It was just in this liberation from history that the opportunity was sensed to lie. (Though Fitzgerald sensed that not even Americans are liberated from history; they are chained to their own myth of having been liberated.) Williams saw, more accurately than anyone, that freedom seized on these conditions entailed nothing less than a separation of words from their speakers, who persist as colloquial "fields" but vanish as persons. In novels, of course, they cannot quite vanish. Fiction's forms are very conservative, not only through courtesy (or anxiety) concerning what readers expect, but in consequence of its offer to show us people saying and doing what they say and do. So Hemingway's morality of style feels positively Victorian (as it is; it derives from the Victorian Underground), and saturnine Nick pervades *Gatsby* like a conscience, and the folk persona toward which the logic of his manner pushed Faulkner is a great judge of dam' foolishness.

Since Faulkner's death, though, the American novel has been yielding to that sense of the arbitrariness of language that provided the poets' opportunity of the 1920's. An early symptom was the welcome accorded Nabokov, for whom the New World was even newer than it was for the first settlers Williams used to imagine, and whose response to its freedoms was to demonstrate that writing a novel can be approached as one approaches an intricate game. Pynchon and Barth among others have since played such games, and Barth has suggested that playing games by one's own rules is the way to go, mainly because many old rules are used up. In "The Literature of Exhaustion" he cites among other gestures "Robert Fillious's *Ample Food for Stupid Thought*, a box of postcards on which are inscribed 'apparently meaningless questions' to be mailed to whomever the purchaser judges them suited for," and "Daniel Spoerri's *Anecdoted Typography of Chance*, 'on the surface' a description of all the objects that happen to be on the author's parlor table— 'in fact however [Barth is quoting from a catalogue] a cosmology of Spoerri's existence.' " Barth's suggestion appears to be that such phenomena annotate the *Zeitgeist*, challenging the novelist to come up with one good reason for not being similarly zany.

Certainly, something has altered since the 1920's. When the poets took over the terrain of the arbitrary, it was never with such lab-coated reasonableness, such courteous explanations that if there was no place to go but the moon, still it was better than nothing. Transported there, the nature of fiction seems to change more disconcertingly than does that of poetry. Why does the infinite possibility that stretched before Williams signify in the imagination of John Barth "The Literature of Exhaustion"?

Probably because of the novel's very scale: because of that, and because it must somehow manage "characters." When we sense that word cards are being dealt, we sense too that the people fiction bids us imagine are no more than the products of combinatorial patterns. Whatever goes in, satire is what comes out. And when the arbitrary game is played for the duration of four hundred pages instead of four, we experience, not as in poems an intensification of our attention, but a reduction: a texture of randomness.

Books of random-number tables have been printed, computer-generated because it is so difficult for the mind to avoid unwilled patterns. These books, and the intricate rules by which the machines that print them out must be instructed (for by what laws may we specify the lawless?), are among the idiosyncratic curiosities of our age. A great order, paradoxically, underlies them. Thus embedded in a random sequence in one such book we find the pentad "44844." It is in place there because to forbid a symmetry of 4's would be to impose a trimness alien to the very concept (concept!) of the random. The order that underlies *Gravity's Rainbow* (Pynchon) or *The Recognitions* (Gaddis), an order achieved by the writer specifying for himself laws like a programmer's, has a not dissimilar feel. Any momentary resemblance to older fictions is like that symmetry "44844," permitted because it would be over-tidy to forbid it. Stevens wrote in "Connoisseur of Chaos,"

> *A. A violent order is disorder; and*
> *B. A great disorder is an order. These*
> *Two things are one. (Pages of illustrations.)*

Art's oldest ambition is to imitate Nature. Now that men have seen planet Earth from afar, "Nature" has become neither human behavior nor that of winds and trees, but instead the Universe, an order so vast it seems random. Yet "the order that rules music," Zukofsky reminds readers of "*A*,"

> *The order that rules music, the same*
> *controls the placing of the stars and the feathers*
> *in a bird's wing.*

Stars and feathers! And the poem reminds us that Bach

made himself arbitrary rules too, rules that seem to make no more sense than a bracketing of stars and feathers. Though Bach thought that

The parts of a fugue should behave like reasonable men in an orderly discussion,

he was not so enthralled by burgher notions of "reason" as to apologize for a composition whose four generating notes were B, A, C, H. *That*, if you like, was a game. (And H is B natural, but the first B is a B flat. Glad you asked.)

Marrying a box kite to a bicycle, installing a brass box equivalent to sixteen horses, making it fly at Kitty Hawk, that was a game also. Homemade like that plane, the fiction of the arbitrary may be still at the Kitty Hawk stage, momentarily aimless because what do you do once you've, yes, gone up and come down again? It took Joyce to discern that what they'd done was resurrect Dedalus. Our newest knowledges always seem to coincide with our oldest. The Wrights and Blériots of the new fiction may be learning to unlock visions of Babylonian splendor and severity, hoping something of the sort may be true but unable to know it until some future Joyce provides a casual demonstration of order.

Index

A Note About the Author

*Hugh Kenner, professor of English at The Johns Hopkins University, is the author of more than a dozen books on subjects ranging from Pound (*THE POETRY OF EZRA POUND, THE POUND ERA*), Joyce, Eliot and Beckett to Buckminster Fuller (*BUCKY: A Guided Tour of Buckminster Fuller). Professor Kenner was born and educated in Canada, received his doctorate at Yale, and now lives in Baltimore with his wife, Mary Anne, and their children.*

A Note on the Type

This book was set in Monticello, a Linotype revival of the original Roman No. 1 cut by Archibald Binny and cast in 1796 by the Philadelphia type foundry Binny & Ronaldson. The face was named Monticello in honor of its use in the monumental fifty-volume PAPERS OF THOMAS JEFFERSON, *published by Princeton University Press. Monticello is a transitional type design, embodying certain features of Bulmer and Baskerville, but it is a distinguished face in its own right.*

The book was designed by Betty Anderson and was composed, printed and bound by The Haddon Craftsmen, Inc., Scranton, Pennsylvania.